PRAISE FOR
AN INVITATION TO PERSONAL PEACE

"Dr. Mike and Kay have written this book to take you on a journey for achieving your own personal peace. It is a roadmap for you to connect to the bigger picture; your true unique purpose. They have paved the way to target your priorities, set daily goals, action steps and align them with your life's purpose. They are your travel agents to personal peace."

—Mike Litman, #1 best selling author,
Conversations with Millionaires
www.MikeLitman.com

"*An Invitation To Personal Peace*, is the definitive book to start you on your journey to finding peace and tranquility in your life. Dr. Mike Davison and Kay Guzder have made your journey easier by removing the roadblocks that stand in your way. They provide clear-cut methods to educate and enlighten. This book is loaded with strategies, tools, ideas, and profound insights that will allow you to make a transition from where you are now to developing your own personal peace goals. The chapters on random acts of kindness, to paying it forward, to cultivating a compassion and living your life as an instrument of peace are destined to be classic essays on this subject. This book will be my reference tool for achieving my own personal peace. Buy this book, its a treasure."

—Frank Gasiorowski
Mr. 90 Day Goals
www.90DayGoals.com

"It's not often that a book can move me to take immediate action but *An Invitation to Personal Peace* did just that. After an almost 18 year separation from my family of origin, the writing exercises in the book helped me realize that I had reached the point in my life where I could now step back in order to move ahead. A little searching on my part and I was able to find one of my sisters and re-established contact with her. The healing process has begun and I know it was because I was reading the right book at the right time in my life."

—Katherine M. Howard,
MAPC, MSM, LPC, EdD(abd)
www.womenintransitions.com

"Reading this book is an act of empowerment. It will teach you how to cultivate a calm and collected personality, so that you can handle whatever comes your way in life. Dr Mike Davison and Kay Guzder's insights are practical, relevant, fun and easy to implement. I was challenged, encouraged and found myself smiling while reading this book. It's a winner!"

—Nicky VanValkenburgh ,
Syndicated newspaper columnist, Gannet publications.
Director of 20 Minutes To Less Stress, LLC.
http://www.20minutestolessstress.com

An Invitation to

Personal Peace

Guidelines To Help You Move Further Along Your Path

Dr. Mike Davison
Kay Guzder, M. A.

1st WORLD PUBLISHING

An Invitation to Personal Peace

✳

Dr. Mike Davison, Kay Guzder, M. A.

© Dr. Mike Davison, Kay Guzder, M.A. 2007

Published by 1stWorld Publishing
1100 North 4th St. Fairfield, Iowa 52556
tel: 641-209-5000 • fax: 641-209-3001
web: www.1stworldpublishing.com

First Edition

LCCN: 2007924688
SoftCover ISBN: 978-1-4218-9942-8
HardCover ISBN: 978-1-4218-9943-5
eBook ISBN: 978-1-4218-9944-2

Dedication

This book would not be possible without the love and support of my wife, Lisa, and our three children, Jon, Jenna, and Joey. I dedicate this book to you. You are the reason I strive to cultivate the principles of personal peace. I truly appreciate your ongoing love, emotional support and patience while I am working at creating personal peace.

—**Dr. Mike**

This book is dedicated to my family. To you my dear husband Shapoor. You have been my friend, partner and protector throughout our marriage. To my children, Jordan and Katy, you have brought so much joy and richness to my life. I give thanks daily for the love and light the three of you bring to my life. To my chocolate lab, Ty. You know far better than me how to live in the moment, love unconditionally, and find peace and joy in the simple things the world offers.

—**Kay Guzder**

And to you our dear readers, who have accepted this invitation to walk in the world seeking peace…may you find what you seek and carry it with you blessing the earth with your gifts.

—**Dr. Mike and Kay**

Acknowledgments

Periods of stress, challenge and adversity play a part of our lives. One cannot be human without experiencing these emotions, these troubles of the soul. We have had the pleasure and privilege of working with many colleagues and clients who have dedicated themselves to understanding the multiple pathways to personal peace. Although there are too many to name, we owe them a debt of gratitude.

Dr. Mike

I want to express appreciate to two individuals who have impacted me in ways they will likely never know. With the passing of my parents, Frank Gasiorowski and Kay Guzder have become my spiritual father and mother. They have both consistently modeled lives of service and a dedication to spreading peace and joy.

Kay

I want to express my gratitude to some of the people who have joined me in my journey as I co-authored this book. Writing it has been an adventure that began when I received an invitation from my colleague, Dr. Mike Davison to co-author this book with him. I cherish the work that we have done together and the richness this experience has brought to my life. He and my teachers and mentors at the Adler School of Professional Psychology guided me intellectually and spiritually along my journey to personal peace.

My sister Jackie, whose editing helped me craft my ideas and clarify my thoughts without changing the meaning or messages I had written. We have shared so much in our lives and careers as sisters and counselors; it only seems natural that we have shared this experience. Throughout my life, Jackie has been an instrument who has brought personal peace into my life.

The inspiration for the art on our book cover came during a weekend in the mountains of North Carolina spent with artist and friend Susannah Flanigan. She understood as a soul sister the importance of internalizing peace as the canvas on which we create our lives.

Finally, I want to acknowledge my dear friend and mentor, Dr. Jarl Dyrud who was a special gift in my life and will live forever in my heart and memory.

Preface

For a number of years we have both had the privilege of working with a diverse group of people struggling with a variety of life's challenges. During this time we have shared in their pain and confusion, and also in their healing and growth. Both of us have felt honored to be invited into the most intimate aspects of the lives of those we have had the opportunity to serve.

Through our collective work we have concluded that many people feel extremely lonely and isolated in their daily lives. They are searching for a connection to a vision and path that will create a sense of purpose in life and lead to a sense of personal peace. We do not claim to have all of the answers. In fact as therapists and human beings, we are on the same journey; searching for peace in our daily lives. Our experience as travelers in our own life's journey combined with what we have learned while sharing in the struggles and triumphs of those we work with in our professional lives, has given us absolute confidence in knowing that the path to personal peace is available to everyone.

We have written this book taking the role of guides leading the way for our readers who wish to develop a greater sense of fulfillment and purpose. In writing this book we drew from our personal experience and our work as psychotherapists. The maps we use include practical psychological insights and powerful spiritual truths from diverse spiritual traditions.

If you long to experience a greater sense of personal peace in your daily life, this book has been written for you. Our hope is that, just as you might use a guide book to travel in any unknown territory, this book and the practices found within it will serve to help move you toward a greater experience of a peaceful life in which your mind, body and spirit can be refreshed and renewed. We believe that the path you seek leads not to a destination but rather to a new way of experiencing life from a perspective of inner peace.

With Peace,

Mike & Kay

Dr. Mike Davison, Kay Guzder

Table of Contents

❋

III. The Golden Key to Personal Peace: Mindfulness

IV. Attitudes & Actions that Further Cultivate Personal Peace

V. Connecting with Your Big Picture

VI. Relationships of Peace

VII. Widening & Deepening Your Path of Personal Peace

Introduction

This book is based on the premise that striving for a sense of balance and peacefulness is a natural quest for all human beings. It has been our experience, however, that a deep and consistent experience of personal peace eludes many of us at every age and stage or our lives. We believe that there are many reasons why so many of us lack a sense of peacefulness in our daily lives. Some reasons are external ones, such as our world becoming ever more complex and fast paced. The result is that we live our lives in a state of turmoil, chaos and confusion and over time, we internalize this chaotic environment and carry the turmoil and chaos inside of us. Our thoughts become like baggage in which we carry feelings of anxiety, fear, paranoia, helplessness and depression. We long to slow things down and live simpler lives with time to pause and reflect on the present moment.

Could it be that personal peace eludes us because we are looking for it in the wrong places? Our culture seems to suggest we focus outside ourselves to find the solutions we seek. The media advertises all around us 24/7 telling us if we buy something, take something or do something that we will feel better. While this orientation can be somewhat useful short term, it seems to lead us to look for an understanding of who we are by following the path of materialism. It teaches us to be outer directed and place blame on others for our lack of feeling an internal sense of peace and balance. Rarely do we search for solutions internally where we find the power to make choices about how to nurture our bodies, minds and spirits.

There are countless other road blocks on our path to cultivating personal peace in our lives. We try, like a rat in a maze to find the way out of our misery. That's because the nature of these road blocks can be summarized as being based on a perspective of self-centeredness. An ego driven approach to life is not natural and creates problematic behaviors and personality flaws as we engage in the "seven deadly sins" of *pride, envy, gluttony, lust, anger, greed and sloth.* Sadly, what is hurt most by these sins is the self.

The pathway that leads us away from an ego driven life is one that looks inward to a deeper understanding of ourselves and our choices. We become aware of our natural desire to be of service to others. In an ego driven life, one's primary focus is on "things" flowing inward to the self. This self-centered approach to life is driven by fear which is the opposite of faith. Faith is necessary for a healthy spiritual condition. Turning inward and rejecting a self-centered approach to living is like reversing the flow of a river. New feelings of peace flow into us and back out again into the world. This book will help guide you to remove the road blocks which prevent you from experiencing your true nature as a person of peace.

What is Personal Peace?

To reiterate our philosophy, we believe all human beings strive for a greater sense of personal peace in their daily lives. Personal peace means different things to different people. However, for the purpose of this book we use the term personal peace as having an internal and external sense of calmness, joy, meaning, purpose, connection with others and connection with something beyond the self.

There are countless tangible and intangible benefits to be experienced by living in a state of peaceful harmony in the world. By mastering the skills in this book, you will learn to use the tools you need to become the person you were created to be. You will live in harmony with yourself and your environment. You will create a new life plan for yourself, one that is not self-centered or even other-centered, but one that is purpose-centered and principle-centered. You will gain a greater feeling of internal and external control of your life. You will be living a life of increased personal satisfaction and direction.

The source of true happiness and personal peace resides within you. Until you allow yourself to fully connect with and pursue your life's purpose you cannot experience true joy and peace. Cultivating personal peace takes courage and persistence. Having a deep experience of personal peace will help you transcend the need for approval from others. It will allow you to be fully present in your life. It will give you a voice to speak your truth confidently. It will put you in touch with your unique gifts and talents. It is the only path that will allow you to live your life authentically as you were meant to live it. The destination is an experience of true happiness which can only be known by finding your personal path to peace.

How to use this book

This book is designed to be used in a number of different ways. It was originally written to be used as a daily guide to incorporate a spiritual practice into your daily life. There are 52 short essays and seven daily practices following each of the essays. The practices are intended to help you apply the concepts discussed in the essays. The purpose of the practices is twofold, while learning new information can positively impact your life, it is the application of the new information that will change your life by changing your thoughts and behaviors.

Another approach to using this book is to choose particular themes of the essays and practices over a day or weekend long solitary or group mini-retreat. It is also a valuable resource to be used by a couple looking to enhance their relationship and create a new context for profound personal and relationship growth. It can be used by parents who wish to create a home in which family members are nurtured daily in a peaceful environment.

Regardless of how you ultimately choose to use this book, you will find that you will benefit most by bringing your whole self into the experience. Like most things in life, it is the level of commitment that will determine your results. Additionally, the consistency of your efforts will be crucial to your growth toward living a peaceful life. In other words, it is not only the cognitive learning of the principles found in this book that will make a difference, but the way those principles are applied in your daily life that will make a difference. Based on this notion, the amount of time you spend on any given day devoted to your own growth and development may be less important than the consistent practice of taking some time on a daily basis to cultivate your spiritual condition.

Dr. Mike Davison, Kay Guzder

Our hope is that you create a powerful connection between the concepts and practices found in this book and your daily life. Our promise is that this level of commitment will deepen your experience of the rewards of living a life based in an experience of personal peace and joy that is the birthright of all human beings.

Finally, we hope that this book will be a catalyst for you to consistently find the time to take a step back and reflect on the one precious moment you have in the one precious life you have been given. Without such reflection there is a high probability that you will get caught in the rapids of a life filled with unimportant trivia that leaves you feeling weighted down with your energy drained and a sense that life has no purpose. Our hope is that by choosing a different path, one of conscious choice to live peacefully in the world, you will connect at a deep level to just how meaningful and precious a gift your life is.

The book is structured around seven sections, which are arranged in an order to best help you allow the principles that will promote personal peace to flow into your life. While you may choose to use the book in any way you find most useful, we arranged the sections in a way that would allow the process to unfold in the most effortless way.

"An Invitation to Personal Peace" is divided into seven sections:

I. **Getting Started on Your Path to Personal Peace.** Take the first step by increasing your awareness of the power within you, and how it can transform your mind, body and spirit.

II. **Removing the Blocks to Personal Peace.** Discover patterns of behavior, tendencies, or shortcomings that get in the way of personal peace. Learn how to remove these barriers quickly, easily and effortlessly.

III. The Golden Key to Personal Peace: Mindfulness. Discover why it's important to be mindful, or fully present in all that you do.

IV. Attitudes & Actions that Cultivate Personal Peace. Discover the motivation for making a commitment, clearing roadblocks, and fostering mindfulness.

V. Connecting with Your Big Picture. Discover the power of contribution, and how to align your priorities, goals and daily actions with your life's purpose.

VI. Relationships of Peace. Discover the power of being consciously interactive with your partner, family and friends.

VII. Widening & Deepening Your Path of Personal Peace. Amplify your experience of personal peace with rituals and healthy mental hygiene.

Once again, it is our deepest desire that this book contributes to helping you develop a life of joy, abundance and personal peace. We sincerely hope that the principles in the book are not merely something you do, but become part of who you are.

✳

Section I. Getting Started On Your Path to Personal Peace

1. Getting started on a path toward peaceful living

"It is only in adventure that some people succeed in knowing themselves—in finding themselves".

—Andre Gide

There is more to getting started on a pathway to finding personal peace than just wishing to live a more peaceful existence. We want to help you identify and examine old thought patterns and fears from the past that no longer serve you so you can move toward the peaceful life style you wish to create for yourself. Why continue to recycle old fears and negative thought patterns that are not enriching your life? They nag at you and rob your energy. The goal of experiencing a sense of personal peace in your daily life is well within your reach. It is a gift you deserve to give yourself.

Before you begin, it would be beneficial to let go of any preconceived notions you have about doing things perfectly on your pathway to peace. On this journey there will be no quizzes or grades given, no judgments or comparisons made. In fact, it is important to make a concerted effort not to place judgments on yourself or make comparisons with others.

Instead, know that this journey will be your unique and special adventure leading to a new understanding of yourself and your ability to bring fulfillment, peace and harmony into your life regardless of your external circumstances.

Have you ever found yourself making the same mistakes repeatedly? Perhaps you've chosen the wrong partner, the wrong career, or given away your personal power. Repeated life lessons are the way that we are called to face and deal with our own particular unresolved life issues. They are the pathway to personal growth and self actualization. Many people trying to solve their problems find themselves embroiled in conflicts rampant with distrust, impatience, dishonesty, disorganization, or intimacy issues, just to name a few. Think about your own personal issues. We have all had these awakenings. Something just doesn't seem right to us and we long for change. Like a pair of shoes that no longer fit, we know it is time to grow because we feel the pinch and the pain that comes from responding to life in ways that no longer suit us. Once we realize our way no longer works, the challenge is to find new solutions and implement them. Fortunately, we are given many opportunities to learn and grow stronger from our repeated struggles as they revisit us and challenge us to face our fears and leave our comfort zone. We can welcome these difficult challenges as opportunities to move toward a more satisfying existence.

When you feel ready, begin to let go of your old boundaries and beliefs. Follow the natural love in your heart that you feel for yourself and others. Your spirit will awaken and seize the opportunities that are waiting for you inside your own creative being. You will be naturally led toward what feeds your soul and spirit and brings you peace.

Daily Practices

Day One: Today choose a quiet place to engage in daily practices. A place where you will not be interrupted. This is a special place where you will read, reflect, write, and complete the daily practices.

Day Two: Today get a pen or pencil, and a spiral bound notebook or journal to take notes. Throughout this program, you are encouraged to write down your thoughts and insights. This will be helpful to track your personal growth, record your successes, and address any challenges you might face.

Day Three: Spend some time thinking and journaling about how you will create the time to do a minimum of 15 minutes of daily reading and practices related to creating peace in your daily life

Day Four: Spend some time thinking about someone who encouraged you, believed in you or made you aware of your strengths and talents. Try to create a role model to emulate.

Day Five: Spend some time identifying the obstacles that have kept you from accomplishing your goals. For example:

"I would like to loose weight, but I am not motivated to eat nutritionally and exercise."

"Ever since I got fired from my job, I have felt like a failure. I am afraid to become vulnerable and try again."

"I keep avoiding a major problem that I know I have to face. I keep putting it off feeling more distracted and scattered as time goes by. I'm spinning my wheels and feeling miserable."

Day Six: Spend some time thinking about your personal battles with negative thoughts. Write down any negative thoughts that you have during the day. List them all in your notebook. Later, look at your list. Reflect and journal about thoughts that have discouraged you and kept you locked into patterns of inactivity and frustration.

Day Seven: Reflect and journal about how you will make this experience different. Strive to do the best you can while having the courage to be imperfect. Focus on the journey and remember the words of Johann Wolfgang von Goethe,

"Trust yourself, then you will know how to live."

Dr. Mike Davison, Kay Guzder

2. Making a choice to change

"Difficulties present choices. We can either waste away from our wounds or we can use them to grow souls."

—Dr. Joan Boryshenko

One of the blessings of my life is that I have had the opportunity to work in a field where I get to meet people from diverse backgrounds. As my clients shared their stories of past successes and perceived failures, I noticed a pattern of behavior that frequently emerged. Many people encountered conflicted thoughts and feelings when they decided to make a change in their lives. While they could easily describe their past successes, they struggled to draw upon past experience to bolster their courage about achieving new goals and challenges. As I looked for ways to encourage them to move forward, I found I didn't have to look far for answers.

Reflecting on my personal experiences with resistance to change helped me to begin drawing a roadmap for clients. I wanted to share with them a way of thinking about making choices, a way that would help them travel down a less rocky path as they move toward their goals. Looking into my "memory mirror" I recalled a time when I was struggling with the idea of returning to graduate school. I talked myself into and out of going to graduate school several times before I ever filled out an application.

I rationalized that I was too old, hearing impaired, over-weight, and too long out of college to remember how to study. In addition to rationalizing, I kept making up excuses that I could use in case my application was rejected. I wouldn't get out of my own way. Regrettably, negative habitual thoughts became by biggest barrier to realizing my dream of becoming a therapist.

However, my dream never faded away. Every time I got back into my comfort zone and talked myself out of going ahead with the plan, I became uncomfortable. Actually, I was downright miserable. It seemed that my old ways of living, thinking and being were no longer satisfying. That's when it dawned on me that my life wasn't working, and it was time to make a change.

I realized that unresolved conflicts have a way of reappearing in life, like those pesky pop-ups on the internet, and no matter how far down into the denial pit you push them, they have a way of showing up time and again. Feelings of being stuck and unfulfilled would cycle around in my head and heart bringing me back to the same place. I could not deny my lifelong dream of becoming a therapist. In order to do that I had to make choices and take actions that would lead me to find my purpose in life and experience a sense of ful-fillment.

To overcome my fears and doubts, I began a practice of positive self-talk. I listened to the positive encouraging state-ments I was creating for myself, instead of the fear based negative rubbish that no longer fit who I wanted to be. I asked myself questions like, "What are you going to be doing five years from now? Five years are going to come and go. Do

I want to stay where I am or move forward?" I asked myself more critical questions like "What would my life be like if I made a change?" "What excuses do I use to avoid making the choices and changes I desire?" "What could be different if I chose to maintain a positive mindset instead of a negative attitude?"

It was then that I began to look at things differently. I realized that I always have choices. I came to the understanding that if I tried to begin a new challenge encumbered with negative thoughts and emotions, I was doomed to failure. I had to stop making excuses, and start thinking about creative ways to resolve my problems. Once I embraced the idea that I had choices, that mindset opened the doors that led to a new way of thinking and acting. I became energized by thinking of my past successes. I remembered achieving many goals that I set for myself in the past. Going to graduate school was just a new challenge for me to face…one step at a time. This mindset gave me the courage to take the steps I needed to realize my dream of getting my graduate degree. It is a decision I have never regretted.

Do you have a dream that you have abandoned or never explored? Are you one choice away from a new beginning? Perhaps you have set aside your deepest desires in order to accommodate everything and everyone else in your life. Are you trying to ignore the whisper that comes in the form of emptiness or restlessness that tells you it is time for change? Like shoes from childhood that no longer fit, growth is a natural part of living and cannot be denied. You can make new choices for your life that can lead you toward fulfillment in whatever you want to achieve. Don't let distractions steal your dreams. Pay attention to those inklings that you've been ignoring. When the "naysayer" appears, either internally or externally, don't join in. Be prepared to cast a vote for yourself. Think about how you will feel five years from now if you don't take a calculated risk. Thoughts and feelings without action never lead to change. Making choices, and following up with the necessary actions, lead to change. Give yourself a chance. Begin to live the life you imagine. Don't go to your grave with your music still inside you.

Daily Practices

Day One: Spend some time reflecting and journaling on your present attitude about change.

Day Two: Journal about past situations where you have regretted not making certain choices or taking calculated risks. What was the outcome?

Day Three: Write a few examples of the things you tell yourself today regarding the choices and changes you want to make. Are you willing to take calculated risks?

Day Four: Write a few examples of past situations in which you made choices that brought about positive results and how you managed to overcome the difficult times. How have you survived difficult times?

Day Five: Write a few paragraphs about how you can apply your past positive experiences to the changes you want to bring about.

Day Six: Is there anything in your life that you would like to change? Even if what you would like to accomplish seems impossible (or just a dream), write it down.

Day Seven: Brainstorm about the action steps you will need to take to get things moving in the right direction. If you don't know how to make thing happen, that is Okay.

Sometimes the starting point is desire. You might feel inspiration or desperation.

> "You don't have to see the whole staircase. You just have to take the first step."
>
> —*Dr. Martin Luther King, Jr.*

3. Exercise your write!

"Writing is the action part of thinking"

—Glenn Dietzel

My friend Glenn Dietzel always says that "Writing is the action part of thinking". It's true. Writing has a way of slowing us down. Writing tends to focus our attention. Writing also enables us to connect with our soul. Some people say that writing opens the door to ideas, thoughts and feelings that are deeply buried in the subconscious. Others say that writing frees the creative muse. In any case, connection with self is imperative in your process of fostering personal peace.

Writing is a powerful personal development and spiritual tool. Writing can help you explore your self, your desires and intentions, and the reasons why you do the things you do. Writing can also helps you live your life more purposefully by externalizing goals and outcomes that are important in your life.

Practice your "write"

Make a commitment to practice your "write". There are countless ways to use writing as a tool for personal and spiritual development. Try "free writing" or writing down

Dr. Mike Davison, Kay Guzder

whatever comes to mind, without judgement. You don't have to share it with anyone, and you can. Write a poem or a letter. You don't have to mail it to anyone, and you can. Write a short story. You don't need to try to get it published, and you can.

What you write is for your eyes only, unless you choose to share it with others. Consider writing a letter to your current self from your child self. Sound corny? Try it anyway. What did you need to know back then? What did you need to hear or experience from someone back then? Write a letter to your future self. Consider writing your own eulogy. While this may strike you as morbid, this exercise can enable you to get in touch with your purpose in life and the kind of lasting impact you want to leave in this world.

Daily Practices

Day One: Psychologist James Pennebaker has conducted countless studies on the power of journaling. Some of his findings include:

Writing thoughts and feelings about trauma or crises for as little as 15 minutes a day, for as few as four or five days, have been shown to be correlated with:

* ✳ College students who journaled visited the student health center less often.

* ✳ An increase in T-cells (optimal immune system functioning).

* ✳ Increased likelihood and rapidity of getting a new job after being laid off.

* ✳ Reduced anxiety and depression.

✻ Improved grades.

✻ Improved mental and physical health of grade-school students, people in nursing homes, arthritis patients, medical students, rape victims, new mothers, and prisoners.

Spend 15 minutes writing about an issue that is on your mind these days. Remember, you are writing for your eyes only. Upon completion of the writing session. Close your journal; Don't review your entry.

Day Two: Like yesterday, spend 15 minutes writing about an issue that is on your mind these days. Again, you are writing for your eyes only. Upon completion of the writing session close your journal; Don't review your entry.

Day Three: Think about your writing exercise from the past two days. Did your writing lead you to a new conclusion or perspective? Review what you wrote. Did you experience a sense of distance, perspective, closure or expanded sense of options, choices or solutions?

Day Four: Write a letter to yourself as a younger person. Particularly at a time that you were going through a difficult time. Give yourself the nurturing, comfort or advice you wish you had received at the time.

Day Five: Write a letter to someone who has hurt you in the past. It may be last week or last year or ten years ago. Remember you are writing for your eyes only. Don't feel like you need to censor what you are writing about. Say everything you need to say or wish you would have said.

Day Six: Write a letter to your future self. Congratulate yourself for having completed or accomplishing what you set out to.

Dr. Mike Davison, Kay Guzder

Day Seven: Write a letter from your future self to your present day self-thanking yourself for being willing to do what you did to succeed.

4. Believing

"Believe in yourself, that you are going to be successful"

—Raleigh Pinsky

I've got a secret and it's time to tell it. For many years I was afraid to pursue my talents and dreams. I was afraid if I put my dreams out there for everyone to see, then I would have to follow through. I was afraid that I just couldn't measure up. As I mentioned earlier, I told myself I didn't have what it takes to get admitted to graduate school and become a therapist. I didn't want to let anyone know that this was my lifelong dream.

I told myself I wasn't smart enough or young enough to get admitted. I was afraid of rejection. I was even more afraid I would get accepted and then what would I do? What if I got admitted, earned bad grades and flunked out? I made up excuses about what I would tell my friends and family when I quit graduate school because the inevitable had happened, I had flunked out. Thanks to my negative belief system, I remained focused on the only possible outcome I could imagine, which was failure. I kept drifting along somewhere between visualizing myself sitting in classes and enjoying them immensely and seeing the nightmare of walking out of

40 Dr. Mike Davison, Kay Guzder

the doors of the university as a dejected and deeply shamed failure. I let my conflicting belief systems take me up and down and around the bend like a roller coaster that kept circling around making me sick! Every time I decided to give up and forget the whole thing I found myself confronted with my overwhelming desires. I couldn't reconcile what I believed about myself as an adult with how I viewed myself as a child.

As a child I wasn't a quitter. I had a deep reservoir of courage. If I fell down, I got up again. I always joined in all the games and was never sidelined by the hard knocks. I was determined to learn about the things I was interested in. I had a keen sense of curiosity about the people, places and things that I saw in the world. I was a determined little kid who never gave up. But who had I become? My adult self was a complete opposite of my child self. I was plagued with self doubt. Funny how I was a lot happier as a child! I finally had to face facts. My adult beliefs had me living in a state of self defeat. I tried to justify my inaction by telling myself that the life I was living wasn't so bad After all, I was surviving. But inevitably my comfort level would be disrupted by a nagging inner voice that told me to stop sugar coating my beliefs about my life. Yes, I was surviving, but I wasn't thriving. I was bored and had lost my zest for living. I struggled with this conflict about surviving versus thriving from high school to college. During that time no one knew my secret. To the outside world I projected myself as a happy-go-lucky person while inside I was feeling miserable. You may be expecting me to tell you that some miracle took place that changed my life. If this were a Hollywood movie it would be scripted to have a magic moment or relationship that suddenly shook me out of my malaise. But this isn't Hollywood and I'm glad that it didn't happen that way. It took a lot of time for me to learn to believe in myself and be willing to risk failure to realize my dreams. Nobody was going to come knocking on my door and hand me an invitation to make my dreams come true. It took soul searching to find ways to dispute my negative belief system. I had to confront my fears so I could be true to myself. For a while, I had to learn to trust other people's assessment of my abilities until I could learn to trust myself. I learned to turn to my friends and my family as a safety net and support system when I did get admitted to graduate school at the age of 52. I learned to take one day at a time, one course at a time, one semester at a time and against all odds, I graduated three years later with a Master's degree in Counseling Psychology.

I can't say that there weren't scary times along the way because there were. Many times I would start to seriously consider going back to my prison of self doubt. However looking back at that place, I was reminded of how scary it can be to stay stuck in your comfort zone and keep your dreams imprisoned. If I kept doing the same things, I'd get the same results. That's why I needed to step out in faith.

I have a hunch there are many of you reading this book stuck like I was in mind-numbing situations. Perhaps you feel trapped in unfulfilling jobs or relationships, and are afraid to take those first steps, afraid to make a mistake and risk failure, so you give up on your dreams. I want to encourage you to put aside your negative beliefs. Ask yourself some empowering questions:

* "What do I want to change about my life?"

* "What do I want to accomplish?"

* "What is stopping me?"

* "How do I begin?"

Answer as if you were listening to the person who most encouraged you as a child. Perhaps it was a teacher, a parent, or a relative. If you can't think of anyone that encouraged you in your childhood, perhaps you can think of a famous person you admired. Picture the person who inspired you to believe that you could do anything you put your mind to if you would only take one step at a time. Ask yourself what they would tell you if you could share your dreams and fears with them. Would they encourage you to forge ahead? Would they tell you not to worry about making mistakes along the way? They would probably remind you that you learn as much from mistakes as you do from success. Listen to the wisdom of the inner voice that tells you that mistakes are opportunities to learn and grow. Mistakes are not reflective of your character or abilities.

On my soul searching journey I chose to revisit times in my childhood when I spent time with my favorite aunt. She was never judgmental or critical of me. She sustained me when I would begin to doubt myself. She would have been very disappointed to hear that I had failed to try. She would not have been critical if I failed, but only if I had failed to try.

Reach into your memory bank and hear the words of encouragement that a special person said to you. Once you do, embrace their belief in you to find the courage to pursue your dreams. There is no better feeling than reaching inside yourself and finding your wellspring of courage. By believing in yourself and your abilities you will come to know your best self and find out what you are truly made of. You'll find that you can empower yourself to manifest your dreams no matter how long or how deep they have been buried. Remember you have faced other challenges in your life and have overcome other obstacles. Thank about what it was like when you were a child and dreamed of becoming a dancer, a fireman, a major league baseball player, or a singer. Don't go to your grave with your dreams in prison. Believe in yourself and your capacity to sing the song of your heart.

Daily Practices

Day One: Consider this quote from Dr. Wayne Dyer's Book "Staying on the Path" *"Our beliefs about ourselves are the single most telling factors in determining our success and happiness in life."*

Spend a few minutes thinking about the above quote, then pick up your journal and write some sentences that you feel best describe what you believe about yourself.

Day Two: Spend some time thinking about changes you want to make in your life. What dreams have you given up on that you want to bring alive? Make a list prioritizing the dreams that are most important to you.

Day Three: Think back to a time in your childhood or young adult years to when you were struggling with a challenging situation. Visualize yourself with the person you turned to who gave you good advice and counseled you to believe in yourself to forge ahead. Write a few paragraphs about that challenging time and how you resolved it. What was the outcome?

Day Four: Spend 15 to 30 minutes doing this exercise in your journal. At the top of a page write a sentence or two about a dream that you have that has not been realized in your life. Now draw a line down the middle of the page. On one side write all the negative thoughts that have interfered with you realizing your dream. On the other side of the page write some positive encouraging statements related to your dream and making it a reality. Ask yourself, "What can I do to make this happen?" Brainstorm and write down all ideas without being critical or judgmental.

Day Five: Re-read the positive statements that you created in yesterday's exercise. Try to visualize an action plan to begin to manifest your dreams in your life. Write down the steps you are willing to take to put your new plan in to action.

Day Six: Ask yourself whether you surround yourself with people who are encouraging and supportive or are your friends "emotional vampires" who drain you with their gloom-and-doom negativity? Identify the people who are on your side. They are the ones who want you to be happy and succeed. Keep them close to you as you begin to take steps to realize your dreams. They are your personal cheerleaders and fans. Avoid people who are negative and try to dissuade you. Write down some specific ideas of how you will keep yourself from falling back into old negative patterns by creating an internal and an external support system. Think about the firemen and rescue workers who go out to work every day. They wouldn't think of leaving behind the tools and equipment that help them do their job and keep them safe. Practice that kind of self-care and self-protection.

Day Seven: Spend some time alone either sitting quietly or taking a walk. Visualize yourself taking the necessary steps to accomplish your goals. Do you see yourself in this new set of circumstances? Try it on for size and see how comfortable you feel. Ask yourself if you would want to go back to the old ways or want to continue on your new more authentic path? When you feel ready, write a few paragraphs to encourage to yourself to maintain your new belief system.

"To dream anything that you want to dream, that is the beauty of the human mind. To do anything that you want to do, that is the strength of the human will. To trust yourself, to test your limits, that is the courage to succeed."

—*Bernard Edmonds*

Dr. Mike Davison, Kay Guzder

5. You are what you think

Q: *What one word should I carry with me for the rest of my life?*

—Peter B. Bloom

A: *Observation!*

—Milton H. Erickson

In today's hurried world we are forced to keep pace. Like the March Hare in Alice in Wonderland, we hear a theme song running through our minds, "I'm late, I'm late, for a very important date, no time to say hello goodbye, I'm late, I'm late, I'm late, and I'm late." With all that we are called upon to accomplish at work and home, it is hard to find time for introspection. However introspection is just what we need. We must find time to get in touch with our thoughts since they shape our attitudes and perspectives. Our thoughts are what drive us toward (or away from) goals and actions. It is easy to go on automatic pilot and respond to the demands and crises of everyday living. Like a runaway train, you may be getting off track and further away from living the life you want for yourself. In order get back on track, you may need to step on the brakes. Take a reading of your internal compass to make sure you are going in the direction you want in life rather than getting derailed. Have you ever gone online to find directions with MapQuest? It may be time for you to do an internal "mapquest".

Here is how to get started. Pay attention to the automatic thoughts that go through your mind on a daily basis. Take a moment to listen. Listen to what you are telling yourself. What thoughts are driving your feelings and actions? Don't try to control or change these thoughts, just observe and make note of them. Be still and become aware of the ways you talk to yourself. You may be surprised to learn that these thoughts are what you are choosing to focus on, and they are driving your actions and choices. In other words, your thoughts create your reality. Everything we think, speak and hear influences how we feel and react in our lives. In fact, we create our own reality. We become what we think, what we dream and what we fear. If we listen to an internal dialogue that is filled with negative self talk, we end up feeling discouraged and defeated. If we listen to an inner voice that is full of fear and foreboding we tend to get stymied and stuck. If we tell ourselves that life is not fair, we feel victimized by others and have the tendency to dwell in self pity. Any of these negative mindsets are self defeating. Negativity stands in the way of our ability to foster self-determination and empowerment. Why would anyone want to maintain a mindset that leaves you feeling paralyzed and stymied? Perhaps you just keep operating out of old habits and patterns, putting your head down, working hard, and not even realizing that you get to choose the path your life is taking. Perhaps in the past you learned to play the role of "the good son or daughter," or "the people pleaser". In acting out that role you unwittingly lost your sense of self.

The good news is that we have the power to reprogram and change our thought process. How do we accomplish this?

We simply need to tune in, listen to our pattern of thoughts, become aware of self-defeating messages we tell ourselves and decide to change the old tapes we have been playing in our heads. We can replace A.N.T.S. (automatic negative thoughts) with P.E.T.S. (positive encouraging thoughts).

How to replace ANTS with PETS?

ANTS are pesky little critters. They make little tunnels in your mind and create a distorted self image. The best thing you can do is recognize ants and get rid of them. The first step is to recognize how and what you think Habitual thoughts become attitudes and beliefs that we rarely examine. You may not be aware of it but our thoughts are often the driving force in our lives. Awareness gives us the choice to break out of our old patterns of thinking and replace them with new more useful positive action- oriented thoughts. As we do this we realize our personal power. This power lies within us to make conscious choices as opposed to giving in to our automatic negative thoughts and fears.

The second step is to use visualization, affirmations and writing to cultivate PETS. These proven techniques will enable you to change your thoughts, perspective and reality. Visualization, affirmations and writing are simple daily practices. It is only a matter of choosing to learn them and making them a part of your daily routine. Learn to question how your thoughts create your life and how you can choose to guide, influence and control your destiny. Discover how to break out of the old self limiting patterns and activate a new life plan that fills you with enthusiasm, energy and self empowerment. Concentrate your effort and focus on the following daily practices for a new way of thinking. Use these tools to discover your path to your best self.

Daily Practices

Day One: Spend some time sitting quietly and paying attention to your random inner thoughts. Practice slowing down and learn to listen to your inner voice. Journal about what you heard as you listened to yourself. Were your thoughts positive and encouraging, or was your inner voice critical and negative?

Day Two: Spend some time visualizing the person you would like to be. What does your personal best look like? Are you living a life driven by your strengths or other people's expectations?

Day Three: Spend time thinking about a personal event, circumstance or relationship that you feel conflicted or upset about. Write one sentence in your journal that describes this situation or event.

Example: My best friend has not spoken to me for several weeks since I confronted her about...

Day Four: Write six sentences in your journal describing an event or situation that troubles you.

Example: My best friend hasn't called or visited in three weeks even though she knows I am sad because I lost my pet.

Example sentences that describe how you are thinking and feeling about the event or circumstance:

1. She doesn't really care about me.

2. Everything else is more important to her than I am.

3. I'm silly to be so sad over losing my pet

4. I can't count on her to be there for me.

5. If she cared about me she would know how I feel.

Dr. Mike Davison, Kay Guzder

6. I'm not going to call her first.

Revised positive thoughts:

1. She has been a good friend and I sadly miss her.

2. This loss is harder than I anticipated and I would like her shoulder to cry on.

3. The reason I am grieving is because I loved my pet. Now that it's over, I'll pull myself together and move on.

4. I need to let her know I want to spend time with her now. My best friend may not be able to empathize with my feelings but that is okay. Perhaps I need to find someone else I can talk to about my grief.

5. She doesn't have a pet so she probably doesn't realize how hard this is for me.

6. I'm going to call her and see when we can get together.

Day Five: Read the six sentences you wrote yesterday. Ask yourself what kind of attitude you have, positive, negative or ambivalent (neutral). Write a P, an N or an X for neutral next to each sentence. Afterwards, re-write each sentence, maintaining the basic thought but putting it in a positive framework. (Note: Perhaps you could make two columns and put the before and after sentences side by side.) Write a few sentences about how your feelings and behaviors change when you read your revised positive thoughts regarding your situation.

Day Six: Spend some time journaling about how you can use your positive point of view to problem solve or reframe your perception around the six specific situations you wrote about on Day 4.

Day Seven: Spend time writing down any automatic thoughts that come to you during the day. Remember to guide and re-direct your thoughts toward positive personal choices. Determine whether your thoughts support positive choices by asking yourself, "How's that working for me?" Dr. Phil on TV always uses that statement to encourage people to look at their situation from a fresh perspective. Bottom line, if what you're doing isn't working, stop doing it. Adjust your approach.

6. Respect for all paths

"What makes us different from one another is so much less important than what makes us alike."

—Oprah Winfrey

One of our basic needs as human beings is to have predictability in our lives. Many of us struggle when presented with new ideas or concepts that are different from our way of life and our cultural belief system. We like to know what to expect. We feel more comfortable with the familiar. Have you ever thought about why we criticize others or make snap judgments about them? When we encounter people who look or think differently from us, we may move into high alert status. Sometimes this causes us to put on our battle armor and defend our uniqueness and lifestyle choices. In the end, we are judgmental and critical, and conclude that we are superior to others.

You may have encountered a person who has a great deal of enthusiasm for a new idea or philosophy. They see it as their mission in life to persuade you to embrace their way of thinking. Many people react negatively by becoming annoyed and dismiss the person and their ideas on the spot. Conversely, we might even have the experience of being in the role of the zealot when we want to share ideas that we are excited about with others. Instead of gaining a willing ear we may encounter resistance and lose the opportunity for mutual learning and growth. There is much to be learned from people who are different from us. We don't have to agree with someone to respect them. Remember that it is okay to be different. It is okay to disagree with someone. A healthy approach may be to find common ground. What does a busy business woman have in common with a stay-at-home mother? They are both women. This is how you can relate to others. Build on the things you have in common. This will enable you to live at peace with others.

If you are given an opportunity to enrich and expand your belief system by learning from someone else's experiences, try not to short circuit the experience. Don't interrupt or become competitive by trying to impose your own cultural biases and convictions. Listen with an open mind and heart. Remind yourself that what is right for you might not be right for someone else. Respect your own path while giving consideration to the path that others have chosen. Where there is a mutual exchange of ideas there is the potential to enhance and enrich each other's life experience.

Resist the urge to criticize, in doing so you will enlighten your own path and become a source of light for the path of others. In his book *Total Self-Confidence.*, Dr. Robert Anthony writes, "You can make yourself miserable by constantly judging and evaluating other people. Remember that other people are doing their best. Give them the benefit of the doubt. Having a light-hearted relaxed attitude about other people will enable you to have a healthier outlook on life." Be a light, not a judge.

Daily Practices

Day One: Journal about your feelings concerning the concepts presented in this chapter. Do you have a tendency to judge or evaluate other people? Do you think of yourself as better than other people? Is your outlook and attitude working for you or do you need to make a change?

Day Two: Journal about a friend or family member who is different from you. What do you have in common? What common ground can you build on?

Day Three: Recall an experience where you responded positively or negatively to someone who is different from you. Spend some time writing about this in your journal.

Day Four: Journal about an idea that you are open to. Write about an idea you feel threatened by.

Day Five: Journal about how you would like to interact in future encounters with people who are on different paths than you.

Day Six: Spend some time reflecting and journaling about how you present yourself when sharing your ideas with others. Are you passive, aggressive or respectful and a good listener?

Day Seven: Spend some time writing in your journal answering the following question: "Am I critical and judgmental of others or am I a source of light and encouragement?"

"You have to be careful about being too careful."

—*Beryl Pfizer, writer*

7. Embracing silence

"Desiderata"

"Go placidly amid the noise and the haste, and remember what peace there may be in silence. As far as possible without surrender be on good terms with all persons....."

—Anonymous

Silence is golden, but trying to find a quiet moment for silent reflection in our fast paced daily lives is almost as elusive as winning the lottery. While silver and gold are considered to be valuable commodities throughout the world, another valuable commodity is frequently overlooked; the value of our emotional currency. In this area most of us live in what resembles a state of bankruptcy. We find ourselves spent at the end of the day with little left to give our loved ones. It could also be said that we don't make time for ourselves. Like an overdrawn bank account, there is nothing left to spend.

Imagine an airplane full of passengers, all seated and ready for take off. Passengers are told what would happen in case of an emergency. An oxygen mask will drop from the ceiling and they should put their own masks on before helping others. In other words, we must take care of ourselves first, before taking care of others. What good are we if we are lying on the floor passed out? By the same token, what good are we to ourselves or others if we are emotionally depleted, overworked, over stimulated, and strung tight as a violin string? A violin string with too much tension will break. A string that is too loose is limp and useless, but finding just the right amount of balance between tension and flexibility cause beautiful music to comes forth. By finding a balance between stimulation and contemplation we can be in tune with our lives. We must learn to value both our need for activity and rest, as both are essential to our well being.

Do you ever find yourself driving in your car listening to the radio as it endlessly repeats newscasts, weather, traffic reports and sports statistics while you simultaneously think about upcoming meetings and "to do" lists, and juggling a cup of coffee and a cell phone? Do you find your mind wandering as you listen to loud music driven by constant beats competing with truck noise, sirens, jet planes, honking horns, and the hits just keep on coming! Much of the time we arrive at our destination not even knowing how we got there. When was the last time you turned off the radio and tuned into the peaceful silence engulfing you in the personal sacred space of your car? Could you perhaps take notice of the blue skies above, the wild flowers by the wayside or the smiling children in the cars around you? Would it be possible to imagine yourself taking the time to proceed in complete silence for the duration of your ride reaching your destination energized and calm? If you can imagine this scenario, you are well on your way to experiencing the enchantment found in the sounds of silence.

By claiming moments of silence in our everyday lives we can attain balance. We will have the energy we need to earn our valuable economic currency and have time to cultivate our emotional currency. Can you take some time to nurture yourself and invest in adding to your emotional bank account? Tend to your own soul first and you may find that you are connecting in a more satisfying way with the souls of those you love.

Daily Practices

Day One: Spend some time thinking and journaling about how and where noise pollution invades your daily life and robs you of emotional energy.

Day Two: Spend some time today noticing of how frequently distractions cause you to operate on automatic pilot in your daily life.

Day Three: Spend 15 minutes reflecting and journaling on how to begin making small changes in your daily life to eliminate distracting noise and stress from your environment.

Day Four: Spend some time journaling on how many times you incorporated periods of mindful silence into your day.

Day Five: Spend some time journaling about how this new technique of personal meditation can bring balance to your daily life. Keep in mind that you can carry this knowledge with you anywhere and own it anytime.

Day Six: Spend some time journaling about all the benefits you have realized by practicing periods of mindful silence. Write about a specific conflict from your past that you would have resolved differently had you known about the practice of mindful silence in times of stress.

Day Seven: Spend 15 minutes journaling about how you felt at the end of the week as you protected and nurtured yourself in a peaceful way. Make note of any changes you have incorporated by paying special attention to whether you added or withdrew from your emotional bank account by experiencing purposeful acts of mindful silence.

8. What does it mean to be spiritual?

"Love the animals, love the plants, love everything. If you love everything, you will perceive the divine mystery in things. Once you perceive it, you will begin to comprehend it better every day. And you will come at last to love the whole world with an all-embracing love."

—Fyodor Dostoyevsky

The words spiritual and spirituality are often used casually. Truthfully, these words are powerful in creating meaning and organizing our experiences. Words are suitcases full of meaning. The challenge is the meaning attached to a word may vary from person to person.

Take some time to define spirituality for yourself. Identify what it means to live a spiritual life or be more spiritual. Admittedly, this is a large task. Take time with it. Allow your own definition to emerge. It does not mean that the definition that others hold cannot be used as a springboard, but you could allow other views to polish your own definition.

For me, spirituality is not religion. Religion can either facilitate or hinder one's spiritual growth. For me, spirituality is not a defined set of rules or practices, although I believe certain beliefs and practices can facilitate one's spirituality.

For me, spirituality is the values I strive to live my life by. Spirituality for me is the way I experience the Divine. Put more precisely, it's how and when I feel the greatest sense of connection to my Creator, who I choose to call God. For me, spirituality is also about feeling a greater level of connection to the world and people around me. For me, spirituality is my sense that I am connected to a higher purpose. It is a purpose that glorifies God, and allows me to more fully use my gifts and talents to serve the community. For me, cultivating my spiritual condition is synonymous with increasing my experience of personal peace. One of the goals of my life is spiritual development. That is, being more loving, less judgmental, and more forgiving.

By no means do the above thoughts encompass all of what spirituality means to me. However, they do capture some of my main ideas. Take the time to define what living a more spiritually rewarding life would look like for you. A destination will never be reached unless it is defined. Admittedly, matters of spirituality are not always easy to define, but do the best you can. Also, keep in mind that there is not a universal definition. Give yourself permission to define spirituality as you travel down your own spiritual path.

Daily Practices

This week, the practices involve contemplative writing. Make use of your journal to document your thoughts. Don't worry about spelling, sentence structure, or even having a clear flow of thought. The benefit of contemplative writing is that it helps you more fully connect with your inner most thoughts, feelings and convictions. It also helps you identify and begin to reconcile areas where you have significant uncertainty.

Day One: Do you believe in God? What is your personal definition of God (and the language use you are most comfortable)? What is the true nature of God?

Day Two: For you, what are differences between spirituality and religion?

Day Three: For you, what is the difference between preachers (or clergy) and spiritual teachers?

Day Four: What does it mean to you to have faith? What is the meaning of life?

Day Five: What are your thoughts about after life? Do you believe in heaven or hell?

Day Six: How do you currently worship? What spiritual practices or rituals you participate in?

Day Seven: Based on responses to these questions, define what it means to be a spiritual person.

9. Be a risk taker

"You've got to go out on a limb sometimes because that is where the fruit is."

—Will Rogers

Many people show up way too small in life. They stay small and settle due to fear. It may be fear of failure, fear of success, or fear of being discovered for the incompetence they feel. Much of the fear of taking risks has long and deep roots. For many, it comes from growing up in a family that sends subtle messages that "you are either with us or against us". In this kind of family, it may have been necessary to downplay, disown, devalue or disconnect from important parts of your being. It reminds me of the old saying that "ships are safest in port, but that is not what ships were built for". Similarly, you were not built to stay small and only express a fraction of who you are.

The big question: Are you ready to venture out? To express yourself more fully? To take risks? There is no better time then the present to begin this journey of risk taking. This does not mean being stupid or acting without thinking things through. Risks can be calculated. Risks can be chunked down into small increments. This all takes preparation and planning. Make a decision to not spend another day paralyzed by fear and indecision. Make a decision to not continue to suffer from the disease of analysis paralysis. The longer you hesitate, they greater your fear becomes.

You may be wondering, what if I stumble and fall? Or you may be wondering what if I fail or get rejected?

Consider these two fears: fear of failure and fear of rejection. First of all, failure is a myth. So-called failure is merely an indication that you need to modify your plan or need more practice. With fear of rejection, most spiritually advanced individuals develop the capacity to rise above the opinion of others. This does not mean that they are insensitive to other people in a general sense. It means they transcend the need to define their adequacy based on the opinions of other people.

This may sound a bit scary. As will all of these topics, you go at your own pace. Personal and spiritual development is not a race or a competition. Find strength in developing a support system. Find strength through prayer. Healthy risk takers accept that in attempting to accomplish your goals and dreams you may need to make mid-course corrections. You may need to start over.

Taking healthy risks with your personal growth means transcending the need for guarantees before you take action. Seeking out too much assurance typically leads to a litany of excuses for avoiding any action. Don't succumb to that internal conversation that tells you to stay small and not risk so-called failure.

Unfortunately, expanding your sense of self and beginning to take risks may disrupt certain relationships. As counselors, we have seen this countless times. The people who love us most may at times be the loudest in their warnings about taking risks. Remember, they have their own fears. However, accepting their warnings without critical analysis means staying small. Please keep in mind that the deathbed literature indicates that people's greatest regret at the end of their life is what they did NOT do, not what they did and failed. Save yourself the later despair. Get out there and stretch yourself toward you most desired outcomes.

Daily Practices

Day one: Read the following poem and reflect on the meaning you take from it. Use your journal to write your reflections.

LIFE IS A GIFT, by Mother Theresa

Life is an opportunity, benefit from it.

Life is beauty, ... admire it.

Life is bliss, ... taste it.

Life is a dream, ... realize it.

Life is a challenge, ... meet it.

Life is a duty, ... complete it.

Life is a game, ... play it.

Life is a promise, ... fulfill it

Life is sorrow, ... overcome it.

Life is a song, ... sing it.

Life is a struggle, ... accept it.

Life is a tragedy, ... confront it.

Life is an adventure, ... dare it.

Life is luck, ... make it.

Life is too precious, ... do not destroy it.

Life is life, ... fight for it.

Day two: Read the following poem and reflect on the meaning you derive from it. Use your journal to write your reflections.

ANYWAY, Author Unknown

People are often unreasonable,

illogical and self-centered.

Forgive them anyway.

If you are kind,

people may accuse you

of selfish, ulterior motives.

Be kind anyway.

If you are successful,

you will win some false friends and

some true enemies.

Succeed anyway.

People may cheat you.

Be honest and frank anyway.

What you spend years building,

someone could destroy overnight.

Build anyway.

If you find serenity and happiness,

they may be jealous.

Be happy anyway.

The good you do today,

people will often forget tomorrow.

Do good anyway.

Give the world the best you have,

and it may never be enough.

Give the world the best you've got anyway.

You see, in the final analysis,

it is between you and God.

It is never between you and them anyway.

✳

Section II. Removing Blocks to Personal Peace

10. Transcending self-delusions

Denial ain't just a river in Egypt.

—Mark Twain

Accurate self-examination is an important part of one's personal growth. It is so easy to fall into self-deception. As counselors, we certainly have fallen into a pattern of not looking at ourselves in a objective manner.

In my clinical work, I have worked with many individuals who had all the markings of success, yet had major pockets of behavior that were inconsistent with their own self image or the view others held of them. Some extreme examples I have seen include the highly respected minister who is addicted to pornography. The accomplished surgeon with a serious drug and alcohol problem. Self-deception makes perfect sense. It is our attempt to make life easier. However, the reverse is true in the long run. Self-deception forces you to live a lie.

Of course, you can not grow spiritually by burying your head in the sand about certain issues, behaviors or aspects of life. You cannot develop a healthy sense of self when you have a self-serving and false appraisal of yourself. Do yourself a favor and be honest with yourself. Conduct what they refer to in the 12-step community as a "searching and fear-less moral inventory." If you are not honest with yourself about certain matters, then doubts and fears will haunt you.

In addition to conducting a "searching and fearless moral inventory," it is crucial to conduct a daily inventory. Ask yourself, "What did I do right today?" and "What did I do well today?" and "Where did I fall short today?" Having a period of quiet time each day allows the opportunity for contemplation and honest self-appraisal. Ultimately, the daily inventory is to determine if you are thinking, behaving and relating with others in a way that is in line with your convictions and those around you. Make this time of self-reflection a daily ritual. As strange as it sounds, pay close attention to yourself. This awareness, coupled with a spirit of humility, may be one of the greatest character building practices you can develop.

Daily Practices

Day one: Denial is a form of self-deception. It can prevent personal and spiritual development, as it prevents us from seeing things as they really are. Use your journal to describe denial that distorts the way you look at yourself or an aspect of your life. Has this halted your spiritual growth?

Day Two: Identify at least one situation you have avoided confronting in your life.

Day Three: Identify what is getting in the way of confronting and/or addressing this issue(s). It is likely a thought or a feeling.

Day Four: How would confronting this issue enhance your life?

Dr. Mike Davison, Kay Guzder

Day Five: Who is a safe person you can get honest with about this issue(s)?

Day Six: Today make a commitment to get honest with at least one other person. Write a script of what you will share with them. Also include in your script what action steps you are willing to take, what input you need from this person, and how they can be a source of accountability.

Day Seven: Conduct the conversations mentioned in Day 6. Denial is all about self-protection. However, it clearly is a trick we play on our self to avoid pain. This trick may work in the short term, but it could also lead to increased pain in the future. Socrates wrote, "The unexamined life is not worth living". Unacknowledged problems do not go away. Be courageous today and have this important conversation.

11. The art of forgiveness

"The weak can never forgive. Forgiveness is the attribute of the strong."

—Gandhi

The practice of forgiveness is at the heart of any spiritual program. Keeping in mind that your spiritual path, albeit deeply personal, impacts the broader human consciousness field.

Forgiveness is restorative. Hatred, or a lack of a forgiving spirit, can keep people stuck in a cul-de-sac of misery. So-called "justified resentment" is entirely incompatible with, and will block you from, the experience of personal peace.

Sometimes it feels like forgiveness is impossible. Remember, forgiveness is always a personal decision. Not an easy decision, but a decision none-the-less. Forgiveness is a decision that goes against our natural instinct of the ego, to "punish" wrongdoing or evil. The act of forgiveness goes beyond a mere giving up resentment, yet that is important. The gift of forgiveness is always necessary for personal healing and peace. Forgiveness is a central message of all of the world major systems of religions. Ultimately, it is only through forgiveness that we can be released from our own hurts and

Dr. Mike Davison, Kay Guzder

misery. It is only through forgiveness that we can be a source of joy, love and peace for others.

Forgiveness is NOT

* Forgetting

* Condoning or excusing the other person's behavior

* Avoiding "the" issue

* A dispensation of consequences

* Necessarily for the benefit of the other person

* An act of self-sacrifice

* Automatically or necessarily ever followed by reconciliation

* A process that leads to immediate freedom from feelings of hurt or loss

Forgiveness IS

* A CHOICE

* Indication of self-care

* Breaking the past's stranglehold on you

* Moving beyond the need to punish the other person

* Moving forward

* A process (NOT an event)

Daily Practices

For several of these daily practices, it will be important to think of someone who you are struggling with forgiving. Another alternative is to think about someone who it took a long time for you to forgive.

Day One: Figure out the payoff for not forgiving. While this may be uncomfortable to look at, hanging on to old hurts can have what psychologists often referred to as "secondary gain". Below are some potential payoffs. Write down in your journal the ones that you think might apply to you.

* Need to be right.

* Need to be superior.

* Proof that I was treated unfairly.

* Attention.

* Sympathy.

* Avoid taking responsibility for my own current actions.

* Excuse for being stuck in life (or at this moment).

* Sense of control from being the punisher.

* Avoid looking at you own part.

* Others?

Day Two: Another process is to figure out the price you pay for not forgiving. This can also be a strong motivator to move toward forgiveness. It can help you more fully recognize who is really being hurt by your un-forgiveness. SOME possible consequences include:

* Lost productivity.

* Feeling consumed or run by feelings of hurt, anger and rage.

* Health consequences.

* Sleep problems.

* Lack of perceived ability to "move on".

Dr. Mike Davison, Kay Guzder

✻ Inability to enjoy previously cherished people, places or experiences.

✻ Others?

Day Two: Another process is to figure out the price I pay for not forgiving. This can also be a strong motivator to move toward forgiveness. It can help you more fully recognize who is really being hurt by your un-forgiveness. SOME possible consequences include:

✻ Lost productivity.

✻ Feeling consumed or run by feelings of hurt, anger and rage.

✻ Health consequences.

✻ Sleep problems.

✻ Lack of perceived ability to "move on".

✻ Inability to enjoy previously cherished people, places or experiences.

✻ Others?

Day Three: Identify a list of what you personally would stand to gain from the process of forgiving. Hint, hint. It might include the opposite of the above list from yesterday's practice.

Day Four: Write a letter to someone who has wronged you. You are writing this letter for your eyes only. Specifically identify what had lead to the feelings of betrayal, hurt or anger. Acknowledge your own part, if you played some part. (Certainly there are times that you did not have a part.)

Day Five: Once you have written the letter, consider some sort of "closure ritual". While this may sound strange, we use rituals all the time to help us navigate through life. Some of them are tied into our culture, some our religion, some our family. They provide us with a sense of connection and certainty. It is also a way to dramatically anchor in a sense of closure and commitment to move forward through a novel experience. Consider burning the letter. If you are not comfortable with burning the letter, put your brain on curiosity mode to help you identify a ritual that is right for you.

Day Six: This exercise is focused on moving toward forgiveness with people you have hurt. Use the 12-step process of making "a list of all persons we have harmed, and become willing to make amends to them all" (Step 8). This involves putting your pride aside and moving past the seductive trap of blaming others. After all, taking responsibility is the opposite of anger. Anger and resentment communicates, "It's your fault". A very brief framework to think about harm you may have caused others includes:

* **Material wrongs:** This includes actions that have impacted another in a tangible way.

* **Moral or Ethical wrongs:** This involves actions that violated your own personal code of ethics. While a comprehensive list of examples is beyond the scope of this book, some common examples include affairs, verbal abuse, physical abuse, lying, and financial irresponsibility.

* **Acts of omission:** This is the flip side of what you "did". It includes what you "failed" to do. Common examples would include express appreciation, be affectionate, not encouraging your partner in their own self-development.

Day Seven: Asking for Forgiveness. As the Biblical passage goes, "Ask and you shall receive". While I am uncomfortable taking literary licenses with the Bible, I will just this once. Add the word sometimes or maybe to the passage above. There certainly are times that your readiness to ask will not match the other person's readiness to give. However, don't just sit around and wait. Earn the privilege of forgiveness.

12. Having the courage to be imperfect

"Behind perfectionism there usually lies a fear of mistakes."

—Rudolf Dreikurs, M.D.

Having the courage to be imperfect is a concept that sounds contradictory. Let's ponder it for a while. Consider the following scenario. In elementary school students are encouraged to get the answers right and avoid making mistakes. You probably remember teachers giving papers back with check marks for right answers and red x's for wrong answers. Sometimes next to the incorrect answers was an explanation. There may have even been a critical remark written in the margin. Knowing the right answers may have drawn praise or elicited no remarks at all. While this may sound like a formula for successful learning, it produces feelings of humiliation that are painful for youngsters to experience. Focusing attention on how many answers a child gets wrong and not on what they get right is a formula for discouragement. Think about the message children internalize when these marked papers are returned. It is unlikely that a child feels encouraged, more likely they experience shame, a sense of inadequacy and feelings of inferiority. Children make value judgments about themselves by comparing themselves to their peers. They don't have enough life experience to figure out that a grade is only supposed to tell them what they need to re-study. They tend to see things in black and white and internalize negative feelings about themselves at a very early age. Educational systems based on perfectionism do a disservice to students. Children learn to embrace a spirit of competition rather than cooperation. Wouldn't it be better to teach our youngsters to do their best and consider their mistakes as useful learning tools? There would be no need for comparisons with others and therefore the focus could be placed on learning, not on who is superior or inferior, adequate or inadequate. Many children develop discouraged opinions of themselves in grade school that inform their choices and behaviors for the rest of their lives.

You may be asking how this relates to our search for peace in our lives. In order to maintain balance and be at peace with ourselves we benefit from understanding the concept of striving for perfection while having the courage to be imperfect. Dr. Rudolf Dreikurs, psychologist and author of the book *Psychodynamics, Psychotherapy and Counseling* writes,

"Behind perfectionism there usually lies a fear of mistakes. Our whole culture is mistake-centered. This is reflected in our educational system dedicated as they are to the prevention and correction of mistakes as a means of developing knowledge and skills. This concern with possible future or past mistakes, universal as it is, is based on two fallacious suppositions. First, making a mistake is considered dangerous. But actually dangerous mistakes are rare, the exception rather than the rule. For example, even in driving an automobile only very few mistakes lead to accidents; and only very few accidents result in injury or death. The fatal mistakes form a minute fraction of the vast number which the

Dr. Mike Davison, Kay Guzder

average driver makes almost daily. The second erroneous assumption is that one must consider all possible mistakes in order to avoid them; otherwise one would become careless and make more mistakes. The opposite is true, the more concerned one is with the possibility of making mistakes, the more one is prone to make one. One can be cautious without fear of making a mistake.

Actually making mistakes is unavoidable and the mistake is less important in most cases than what the individual does after he has made the mistake. If he is discouraged, demoralized and beset with guilt feelings, he cannot face the situation as it is. But if he is a courageous person, the predicament may often lead to benefits which would never have been possible without the original mistake. What is needed is not concern with what we have done wrong, but the determination to meet the demands of the moment. One of the causes for our preoccupation with mistakes lies in the competitive strife, making a mistake implies humiliation; it lowers one's social status, as being right increases it. This is at the root of our concern with goodness and righteousness. We are interested in it primarily because we are interested in our own prestige and status. Once we free ourselves from our fear of being inferior and recognize our self worth and dignity, we no longer fear making mistakes- and therefore make fewer. Our educational institutions are not yet prepared to teach this new social value of the courage to be imperfect. The ability to make mistakes graciously and to accept the ensuing predicament in the same spirit as if it had occurred without our fault is essential for functioning as a free person, as an equal among equals."

The paragraphs above illustrates how having the courage to make mistakes allows you to challenge yourself and try new ways of thinking and learning. Ask yourself if you are willing to let go of your old ideas of perceived imperfections and failures. Can you meet yourself where you are and go on from there? Can you tell yourself "what I am is good enough?" Can you embrace the "good enough concept" and apply it to all your endeavors. Can you dispute the old ways of thinking and keep your courage? Courage recognizes failures and mistakes as opportunities for growth. Courage continues taking risks after experiencing mistakes and failures. Courage disconnects from outcome and concentrates on the journey. Courage is the inner voice that says "Do the best you can and let go of your fears." Be open to applying these concepts when you are faced with resolving some mistake you've made or some difficult decision to be reconciled. You may be surprised by what you accomplish. Wouldn't it be worth a try? Do you have the courage to be imperfect and take the risks? Listen to the wisdom of your heart as you read a quote by Mary Anne M.B.L. Radmacher:

> "Courage doesn't always roar. Sometimes courage is the quiet voice at the end of the day saying—I will try again tomorrow."

Daily Practices

Day One: Spend some time reflecting on how your fear of failure or feelings of inadequacy keep you from making the choices in life that you want for yourself.

Day Two: Spend 15 minutes reflecting and journaling about Dr.Dreikurs' concept of how fear of making a mistake and striving to avoid mistakes leads to discontentment.

Day Three: Spend 15 minutes journaling about how striving for perfection has limited your personal growth.

Day Four: Spend some time journaling about your ideas on what it means to take risks and be courageous.

Day Five: Spend 15 minutes writing any new insights you discovered about yourself from yesterdays journaling exercise. Ask yourself, "Am I willing to have the courage to be imperfect to begin movement toward my personal goals.

Day Six: Spend 15 minutes writing about the steps you will take to implement a plan of action.

Day Seven: Choose one personal goal that you wish to accomplish or one problem you wish to solve that you've been avoiding. Write a plan of action. Keep in mind the "good enough concept and have the courage to be imperfect as you work your issues through to resolution. Write in your journal how this exercise helped you and how you plan to apply the concepts to future problem solving and goal setting issues.

13. Acceptance

"There are years that ask questions and years that answer them."

—Zora Neale Hurston

Think about a time in your life when you have faced overwhelming difficulties and heartbreak. Perhaps you were dealing with a situation that brought you to your knees and left you feeling paralyzed with fear, anger or despair. It might have been the death of a loved one, catastrophic illness, divorce, loss of a job, loss of your home or financial losses that threatened your most basic feelings of security. If you think about your own experiences and those of your loved ones, you find that no one gets through life without being confronted by strife. It is called "life on life's terms". When the multiple stressors strike, it feels like we're the only one who ever has experienced such intense pain. It is at these times that we learn to reach deep within ourselves to find the courage, strength and wisdom we need to move forward and survive the turmoil.

Author and Minister Hugh Prather in his book *The Little Book of Letting Go*, reminds us that "We can let go and be free, or we can fight useless battles, but we can't do both!" The lesson here is to learn to let go and accept what we can't control. When we get caught in a web of negative emotions such as anger, blame, and self pity, we are less able to respond to our pain in ways that lead us to healing and resolution. We can choose to walk the path of acceptance by asking ourselves some questions to help lead us away from negative feelings of despair and hopelessness. Ask yourself how the lessons of the serenity prayer (God, Grant me the Serenity To Accept the Things I Cannot Change; The Courage to Change the Things I Can; And the Wisdom to Know the Difference) can guide you. Contemplate the idea that acceptance is the key to living a life of serenity. When you maintain an attitude of acceptance, you can't continue to do battle by holding onto anger and hostility. One will inevitably displace the other.

The next step is to ask yourself to identify the attitudes you hold that contribute to feelings of insecurity and fear. These attitudes block you from the ability to accept things you cannot change. Are feelings of anger, blame and the desire to retaliate keeping you embroiled in a battle? If so, look for ways to soften and open your heart. Cultivate the ability to be compassionate by opening your heart and mind to your own suffering. Embrace and practice loving kindness toward yourself. Expand the concept of loving kindness toward yourself and extend it to others who are suffering from similar painful experiences. By practicing loving kindness toward yourself and others you will move away from feelings of paralysis related to your personal difficulties.

There is comfort in recognizing that you are not alone. Acceptance suggests that there is universality to the human experience. Everyone has heartaches, heartbreaks and mental anguish at some time in their lives as well as an equal share of joy, delight, excitement and pleasure. The Chinese call this looking at the Ying and Yang. Inevitably we all will experience birth and death, illness and wellness, sorrow and joy, good times and bad. We can learn to accept that we all will get a fair measure of life's experiences along the way. When we embrace an attitude of acceptance we open our hearts to the adventure of living. Think about your most painful experiences in the past and ask yourself if these experiences didn't hold the seeds of new beginnings. In retrospect we realize that those things that seemed like insurmountable tragedies somehow got resolved. We grew from what we learned by surviving to greet better times. We may never forget but we do survive and many times the outcome leads us to open doors that we never thought we could open.

It is worthwhile to reflect on the joys and struggles of being human. We all have to contend with difficulties many times in our lives. Each time we stay the course and find the courage to face life's challenges we develop new coping skills. We gain inner strength which fortifies us to see the next battle as not so frightening and overwhelming. We prove to ourselves that we can handle the most difficult situations. We add to our reservoir of personal strength and courage. Acceptance is the key to facing life with courage and confidence. It allows us to be optimists who celebrate life and look forward to each age and stage of life's journey.

Daily Practices

Day One: Spend some time reflecting and journaling about a time in your life when you faced a troubling challenge. Write about your strengths and weaknesses in coping with that situation.

Day Two: Spend some time journaling about some difficult issues that you are currently facing. Determine which ones you have the ability to affect and those that are beyond your capacity to control. They are opportunities to learn about practicing acceptance.

Day Three: From yesterday's practice write a few paragraphs about those issues you feel you can positively impact and the steps you can take to begin the process. On a separate piece of paper write about those issues that you know you cannot change and have to accept realizing that acceptance is the next step to healing and moving on with your life.

Day Four: Spend some time journaling on ways that you can practice developing an attitude of acceptance toward yourself and others. Notice how passing judgments and being accepting cannot co-exist in your heart and mind.

Day Five: Spend some time reflecting and journaling on the concept of accepting the things you cannot change and the courage it takes to reach that point of acceptance. Consider times in the past when you were reluctant to accept the inevitable and how difficult the challenge remained until you got to a place of acceptance.

Day Six: Spend some time journaling about the value of developing an attitude of acceptance in facing one current challenge. Write about the benefits of being free to move on with your life when you're not spending energy trying to control the things you cannot change?

Day Seven: Spend 15 minutes journaling about your capacity to have an open, compassionate heart and mind in dealing with present and future difficult challenges. Ask yourself if you need to have a shift in attitude in order to get to acceptance.

14. Gain freedom by letting go of control

God, Grant me the Serenity
To Accept the Things I Cannot Change
The Courage to Change the Things I Can
And the Wisdom to Know the Difference

This powerful little prayer suggests that serenity comes into our lives when we learn to accept the things we cannot change. It sounds so simple. If you can't change it, you will just have to learn to live with it. Tell that to someone who has just lost a loved one or just learned about a spouse's infidelity, or has a son or daughter hooked on drugs. The human spirit fights to avoid pain by searching for ways to take control and make things the way we want them to be. The truth is that by accepting that we have no control, we must also accept the pain that comes with loss, betrayal and helplessness. We learn to accept that there will be pain and loss in life. When bad things happen we may blame ourselves as a way of taking control of the outcome of situations we can't accept. We use self-talk such as, "If only I'd been a better mother, a better father, a better spouse or friend such a thing

Dr. Mike Davison, Kay Guzder

wouldn't have happened." Or we may tell ourselves "I should have known better. How could I have been so stupid? Anyone else would have known better."

One of the hardest lessons to learn is that most of the time we have no control over the events that occur around us. Nor can we be responsible for the thoughts, feelings, and actions of others. We can only control ourselves and accept other people and the world around us as they are at the present moment. Spiritual teachings tell us that all creation is perfect just as it is. It is not our purpose to dominate it and change it in order to make it better or to make ourselves more comfortable. What a hard thing it is to have faith that if we accept life on life's terms including birth, death, sickness, health, happy times and sad times, that we are gaining freedom and serenity in our lives. When we live in fear it is because we lack faith in ourselves and in a power greater than ourselves. We lack the faith that we possess the skills we need to cope with life's disappointments and tragedies. Instead we long to escape pain by trying to control things that we can't face. It's like trying to swim upstream in a raging river. We get swept away and drown in our feelings of confusion and helplessness.

The late Dr.Elizabeth Kuebler Ross wrote in her book, *On Death and Dying*, that there is a process we go through when we experience loss. The first stage of the process is *Denial.* We refuse to believe that something has been lost. We feel a sense of disbelief and hope that we are going to wake up from a bad dream and all will be well again. The next stage is *Bargaining.* We try to strike a deal with God. It goes something like this, "If you make this bad thing go away, I'll never tell a lie again." We have the illusion that we can somehow regain control over what has happened. The third stage is *Anger.* We rage at God and the situation. "Why did this happen to me?" "It isn't fair!" "Somebody will pay for this!!!" Finally when the anger burns itself out we reach the final stage of grief, which is *Acceptance*. Acceptance allows us to live in the moment and be present in our life coping with our grief and loss.

By incorporating a daily practice of living in a spirit of acceptance of things we cannot change, we can be more present and more appropriate in our response to our losses by admitting that we feel pain. We can reach out to others for comfort. We acknowledge our loss and accept it as part of the natural order of life. We realize that suffering is something that we share with others and so we join support groups for those who have experienced similar losses. This is a much more authentic path that will lead us toward healing and regaining our equilibrium.

The Serenity Prayer also tells us that we must find the "*Courage* to Change the Things We Can." It takes courage to look within ourselves and take an inventory of the ways each of us creates the misery in our lives. One sure fire path to feeling helpless in our life is our tendency to blame others for everything bad that happens to us. Not only does blame lead us to living the role of a victim, but it puts all of the personal power we have in life into somebody else's hands. Consider this statement…I may hate that I am overweight, and blame my parents for giving me bad genes, for feeding me the wrong foods as a child or for not encouraging me to be more athletic but the only way I can resolve the problem is to take charge of my choices each day and replace negative talk with positive action. Perhaps I was born into a family of substance abusers. I can choose to continue the legacy or I can be the chain in the link that breaks the pattern of using alcohol or other drugs and live my life practicing a daily recovery program. I can't change who my parents are, or what family I belong to, but I can change myself and the choices I make each day.

Finally the Serenity Prayer asks God to grant us wisdom. Wisdom is gained through experience. We gain wisdom by learning the lessons that life teaches either through trial and error or by reading and understanding the writings of life's great teachers and philosophers. We learn to forgive ourselves and others for being less than perfect. We learn not to judge others harshly but rather to live authentically according to our values. We learn to live in a state of gratitude for the gifts life gives us every day. We learn to see beauty in simple everyday pleasures. We notice how good it feels to sleep in a clean bed. How wonderful a shower feels as the warm water flows down our backs. We see the birds and listen to their song. We accept that pain and loss are part of life and bring us closer to those who want to comfort us. This is the way that living brings us wisdom. This is how we come to understand and experience a state of living a life of serenity. It means I do not control but rather co-exist at each age and stage of life and be in the world just as it is at the present moment.

Daily Practices

Day One: Spend some time meditating and journaling on the Serenity Prayer and reflecting on what it means to you.

Day Two: Spend some time journaling about areas in your life where you have tried to control things you could not change.

Day Three: Spend 15 minutes identifying what barriers you create that prevent you from letting go of your need to control the things you cannot change. Enter them in your journal as you become aware of them. Examples are fear, lack of trust in others, feelings of superiority.

Day Four: Spend some time identifying ways that trying to control situations and people has hurt others and you.

Day Five: Spend 15 minutes identifying areas of your life that you want to change and that are under your control.

Day Six: Spend 15 minutes journaling about positive steps you will take toward creating serenity in your daily life by letting go of your tendency to control people or situations.

Day Seven: Spend some time journaling about what you are grateful for in life and take time to notice the beauty that surrounds you in the present moment.

Dr. Mike Davison, Kay Guzder

15. Nothing personal

"Don't Take Anything Personally. Nothing others do is because of you. What others say and do is a projection of their own reality, their own dream. When you are immune to the opinions and actions of others, you won't be the victim of needless suffering."

—Don Miguel Ruiz

In a wonderful book entitled *The Four Agreements*, Don Miguel Ruiz suggests to "Never take things personal". What a powerful spiritual concept to implement into your life. Not taking things personal allows you to transcend so many of our human foibles such as the need to defend and justify. The tendency to personalize will keep you in reaction mode. Personalizing is a sure way to block you from accepting people from being who and where they are on their own journey, which is a necessary pre-condition to personal peace.

When I think of transcending this very human tendency to take things personally, I think of all of the times I have walked around like a giant piece of Velcro picking up lint balls from so many people. The energy of carrying this extra baggage around is emotionally, physically and spiritually draining. It takes me out of the moment and keeps me in reaction.

I also think of the childhood saying "I am rubber and you're glue, what ever you say bounces off of me and sticks to you". While this may not sound like the most spiritual saying, I believe it has powerful spiritual implications. Recognizing that people respond and operate out of their own ideas and belief about the way thing "are" or the way things "should be". If people approach me with judgment, I believe that their judgment does not define me. I believe it defines their need to judge. Now be careful not to judge their judging, because even judging judging is judging. Merely observe and take note.

To integrate this practice of not taking things personally is very freeing. It allows us to bypass many hours of the "attack and defend" dance that contaminates relationships. It allows us to transcend the need for retaliation. Ultimately we discover our truest sense of freedom, personal power and peace when we transcend the tendency to personalize or the need to make people or situations other than who, how, or where they are.

Daily Practices

Day One: Contemplate Ruiz's encouragement to "Not Take Anything Personally". Allow yourself to temporarily take on his position that nothing others do is because of you. What others say and do is a projection of their own reality, their own dream. When you are immune to the opinions and actions of others, you won't be the victim of needless suffering.

Today if you find that others want to offer their opinion of you, positive or negative, smile and say, "thanks for sharing." If it is negative, let it become as water off a ducks back. Later take the feedback and determine the personal usefulness for you.

Day Two: Repeat these declarative statements several times throughout the day:

* Taking things personally serves me poorly.

* Taking things personal increases a sense of threat within me.

* Taking things personally sends the message to others that my point of view is flimsy.

* Taking things personally prevents me from learning what I need to learn.

Day Three: Reflect, in writing, on how you tend to respond when you personalize other's behavior. What is that all about? What buttons of yours are being tripped?

Day Four: Expand on your reflections from yesterday. What factors trigger you to personalize someone's behavior? How do you handle when someone challenges or questions your ideas or positions? When you personalize is it more about the challenges or questions or more about your idea or position? Is your tendency to personalize about your relationship with the person issuing the challenges or questions? What other factors contribute to your tendency to personalize?

Day Five: Identify specific ways taking things personal diminishes your effectiveness in the world.

Day Six: Visualize a situation where you took something personal and lead to you getting defensive or less effective in some way. Specifically visualize the statement or situation that you interpreted in a personalizing way. At that specific moment, picture yourself being unfazed by the statement. Picture yourself staying cool and calm and, as in day one practice, imagine yourself saying "Thanks for sharing". You are saying this without sarcasm, but out of a genuine openness to the person perspective.

Day Seven: Visualize a situation that you anticipate occurring in the future where you may be prone to taking things personally. Imagine yourself remaining open and effective without allowing your ego to dominate, which can lead to pettiness, defensiveness and an overall diminished effectiveness.

Dr. Mike Davison, Kay Guzder

16. Feel the fear and do it anyway

There is no fear in love; but perfect love casteth out fear: because fear hath torment. He that feareth is not made perfect in love.

—1 John 4:18

To experience fear is to be human. However, fear can be highly disabling. In my work as a Clinical Psychologist I have met many folks that seem to be run by fear. What you may not know is that fear has a first cousin. It is avoidance. To diminish fear you must face it. An effective way of transcending fear is to 1) acknowledge it, (2) pinpoint exactly what you want to accomplish, (3) break up your desired outcome into small, more manageable steps, and 4) take action. This takes bravery and courage. Acting with bravery and courage is not acting without fear. It is acting in spite of fear.

Another aspect of conquering fear is to associate with courageous people. Find role models who have already done what you are afraid of doing. Observe them. Get their ingredients for accomplishing what they did. What did they say to themselves? What did they do? Now replicate their formula.

Remember that courage is like a muscle. It gets bigger the

more you use it. Remember that fear is learned behavior. Therefore is can be unlearned. With each courageous action there is a diminishing of the fear. Once you overcome fear of a formerly feared action you will experience a great sense of exhilaration.

All this being said, I want to anchor back to my original statement, to experience fear is to be human. If you are not experiencing some level of discomfort at any given point in your life it suggests to me that you are not growing. Expanding your sphere of influence and expanding yourself will come with some mild discomfort to extreme fear. Mild discomfort is easy to transcend. Take the Nike approach. Just do it! With extreme fear small-calculated steps with the support of a trusted person is typically the best course of action.

There are times when simply thinking positively won't move you past your fear and anxiety. There are times when simply plodding through is the thing you must do. You won't stay small by being fearful—you will stay small if you allow fear to immobilize you. So no matter what it takes, keep moving.

Fear is much like a quagmire—it slurps at our feet and if we stand still long enough, it begins to suck us down. It's hard to get out of, but it is possible. Don't allow fear to block you from the joy and personal peace you deserve.

Daily Practices

Day One: Read Our Deepest Fear—an excerpt from the book, *A Return to Love: Reflections on the Principles of a Course in Miracles* by Marianne Williamson. Then contemplate how it applies to your own life.

Our Deepest Fear:

"Our deepest fear is not that we are inadequate. Our deepest fear is that we are powerful beyond measure. It is our light, not our darkness, that most frightens us.

We ask ourselves, who am I to be brilliant, gorgeous, talented and fabulous? Actually, who are you not to be? You are a child of God. Your playing small does not serve the world. There's nothing enlightened about shrinking so that other people won't feel insecure around you.

We are all meant to shine, as children do. We were born to make manifest the glory of God that is within us. It's not just in some of us; it's in everyone. And as we let our own light shine, we unconsciously give other people permission to do the same. As we're liberated from our own fear, our presence automatically liberates others."

For the next several days think of something currently in your life that you have attached fear to when you complete the daily practices.

Day Two: Think of the "source" of the fear. Where did the fear come from? Have you been dwelling on the difficulties instead of the opportunities? Have you been listening to those who are cynics and pessimists, instead of coaching yourself with positive words and people? If so, you may need to move on. You may need to get away from people and situations that drag you down. Externalize your thoughts by writing your answers in your journal.

Day Three: Identify things you have accomplished. Identify ways you were able to accomplish extraordinary things in spite of fear. This will begin to empower you to move forward on a current matter in spite of fear.

Day Four: Take stock of your talents and skills. Fear often tells us that we "don't have what it takes…" Show fear as the liar it is: list your skills, all your positive attributes. Then look at your current challenge again, after you have a new appreciation for your God-given talents and abilities.

Day Five: Don't underestimate the power of prayer. Regardless of your spiritual beliefs, there is an amazing power that comes from releasing your fear to a God Who loves you and is looking out for you. Don't bottle the fear up—let it go. You don't need it anyhow!

Day Six: I have many times heard the acronym regarding fear that it is:

F= False

E= Evidence

A=Appearing

R=Real

That is really what fear is—it is an unrealistic look (false look) at something and attempting to make you believe it (appearing to be real). Identify times when you talked yourself into unnecessary fear.

Day Seven: Identify ways you have restricted your life because of fear. Specifically identify places you have avoided, things you did not do, and people you avoided. Think of how fear generates thoughts of doubt, self-criticism, imagining catastrophic scenarios, which serve to keep you small and restricted.

Dr. Mike Davison, Kay Guzder

Section III. The Golden Key to Personal Peace: Mindfulness

17. Mindfulness

"When we touch out heart in mindfulness we see clearly that a heart in good condition is an element of real peace and happiness and we vow to live in a way that keeps our heart in good condition"

—Thich Nhat Hanh

Peace and calm don't come naturally to us in the frantic pace of our daily lives. We have to make a conscious decision to create a peaceful existence. Our mind is constantly active and in motion with thoughts and feelings running through it. We have a tendency to complicate our lives endlessly. We do things repeatedly when we know it will make us miserable and then we are frustrated when we get the same results. We try to control events in our lives to prevent bad things from happening. Add to this a dash of the "shoulds and oughts", a sprinkling of our "guilts and fears" and mix it with a dose of our "anxieties and inadequacies" and we cook up a batch of trouble. In order to cope with this we shift into our automatic negative ways of thinking, tie ourselves in knots, and then wonder why we are going around with our "undies in a bundle!"

In his book, *The Miracle of Mindfulness* author, philosopher and poet, Thich Nhat Hanh writes, "It is sad that when something happens to us that we don't like, we spend most of our time tensed against that experience and it is already over. It may not happen again but probably something else will. When we are so focused on the past and something in the present feels similar we shift our attention to that, but soon that experience becomes part of the past and then we bump into something else in the present which feels just like those other two experiences. We are always protecting ourselves from experiences that we have had or projecting into the future to prevent them from happening again. All we have is the present and we are not fully active in our own lives when we are past and future oriented. Many people ruminate about what has happened and what will happen as a way of protecting themselves i.e. covering all the bases so to speak, a method of survival, but with staying in the present moment you are aware and active in your own life, then your natural intelligence is in command. Most people have never been hit by cars, their natural intelligence keeps them from stepping in front of a car. Most people who are hit by cars aren't present, and aren't paying attention."

By practicing mindfulness we learn to stay in the present moment and experience life fully. We stay focused and aware of what is happening in the moment. This gives us the ability to think and respond to our lives in ways that are in our best interest. We learn to be still and listen to what our thoughts are telling us about what we need. One could argue that in times of crisis and stress our mind is inevitably distracted so how is it possible to learn to be still, calm and focused? Thich Nhat Hanh would say that it is only through keeping your attention focused and practicing mindfulness that we can handle all the millions of difficulties we are asked to resolve throughout our lifetime. Each of us must attend to work and family obligations while dealing with the unexpected crises and hardships that inevitably occur on a regular basis in our lives. Mindfulness is the miracle by which we master and restore ourselves. Mindfulness is the miracle which can restore our scattered mind to wholeness so that in either bad or good times we are equal to the challenges that life brings to us. By practicing mindfulness and staying in the present moment we are better prepared to meet life on life's terms, celebrate and rejoice in the good times and handle and resolve the complexities and tragedies in times of strife.

How do we learn to be mindful, to be present in the moment, when there is chaos in our lives? Consider this quote by TV celebrity Oprah Winfrey "I've learned that the more stressful and chaotic things are on the outside, the calmer you need to get on the inside." Learning new skills and practicing them will help us let go or our tendency to get anxious and unfocussed when faced with a crisis. One very simple technique you can utilize to gain control and remain calm in stressful situations is to learn the practice of mindful breathing. By rhythmic breathing we bring oxygen deep into our lungs. Mindful breathing helps us to become calm and focused so that we can think clearly how to respond to the situation at hand.

The following example by Thich Nhat Hanh illustrates how to learn the practice of mindful breathing:

"You should know how to breathe to maintain mindfulness, as breathing is a natural and extremely effective tool which can prevent dispersion. Breath is the bridge which connects life to consciousness, which unites your body to your thoughts. Whenever your mind becomes scattered, use your breath as the means to take hold of the mind again. Knowing how to breathe is essential to the practice of mindfulness. Consciously attending to your breathing is the gateway to clearing the mind of distractions and clutter. It is the first step in grasping and staying in the present moment. "Breathe in lightly a fairly long breathe, conscious of the fact that you are inhaling a deep breath. Now breathe out all the breath in your lungs, remaining conscious the whole time of the exhalation. Mindfulness teaches the method to take hold of one's breath in the following manner: "Be ever mindful you breathe in and mindful you breathe out. Breathing in a long breath, you know, "I am breathing in a long breath." Breathing out a long breath, you know, I am breathing out a long breath." "Breathing in a short breath, you know, I am breathing in a short breath." 'Set aside some time to practice mindfulness and breathing. Ideally it would be better to practice on a day when you do not have to go to work. When you awake in the morning while still lying in bed slowly follow your breath, slow, long and conscious breaths. Then slowly rise from bed (instead of getting up all at once as usual), nourishing mindfulness in every motion. Once up, brush your teeth, take a shower and do all your morning activities in a calm and relaxing way, each movement done in mindfulness. Follow your breath, take hold of it, and don't let your thoughts scatter. Each movement should be done calmly. Measure your steps with quiet long breaths. Spend a half hour taking a bath. Bathe slowly and mindfully, so that by the time you have finished, you feel light and refreshed. You may then move onto your daily tasks. Whatever the tasks, do them slowly and with ease, in mindfulness. Don't do any task in order to get it over with. Resolve to do each job in a relaxed way with all your attention. Enjoy and be one with your work. Without this attitude a day of mindfulness will be of no value at all. The feeling that any job is a nuisance will soon disappear if it is done in mindfulness. No matter what task or motion you undertake, do it slowly and evenly without reluctance. If you can find a half day to practice and then graduate to a whole day, eventually the practice of mindfulness will penetrate the other days of the week enabling you to eventually live seven day a week in mindfulness."

Similar to learning a new language, you need to practice the technique of mindfulness in order to gain familiarity with the new concept. By incorporating this practice into your daily life you will begin to experience how it feels to exist in a more calm and peaceful atmosphere. The benefit of practicing mindfulness in your day to day life is that when stressful circumstances arise in times of crisis you will be fortified to respond by staying calm. You will find you have the presence of mind to deal with the situation at hand with a sense of clarity. You will be able to stay focused and problem solve. Your will have trained yourself to utilize this new coping mechanism. Like the Lamaze birthing technique that mothers practice for several months before the birth of their child, we must practice in times when we are not in distress. We want to teach our mind and body to respond automatically during times of pain and stress, to stay calm, focused and capable of handling the critical issues at hand.

Daily Practices

Day One: Spend 15 minutes becoming familiar with the meditation and breathing techniques described above. Practice mindful breathing.

Day Two: Spend 15 minutes practicing the deep breathing techniques. Write a few paragraphs about what you were thinking while do the breathing exercises and practicing mindfulness. What were you feeling?

Day Three: Spend 15 minutes practicing the breathing and mindfulness techniques and notice how each day you become more comfortable and more relaxed in the practice. Don't be concerned if you mind wanders or resists with thoughts of other things that you "should be doing". Let these thoughts drift through your mind and flow out again without paying particular attention to them. Continue to focus on the mindful breathing and relaxation.

Day Four: Spend 15 minutes journaling about what you are learning from your daily practice. Write about a crisis situation that you experienced in the past that you feel you did not handle well. Example: A car accident, an injury to your child, a serious situation that called on you to think and respond quickly at a moments notice.

Day Five: Spend 15 minutes writing in your journal how you will create more time in your daily like to practice mindfulness in order to deepen your understanding and gain more experience with the application of mindfulness in times of crisis. Contemplate how mindful breathing could have made you more effective in that situation.

Day Six: Spend 15 minutes journaling about what you are learning from your daily practice. Write about a past crisis situation that you experienced and try to visualize how you would handle that crisis now since realizing the benefits of practicing mindfulness. Would you feel better prepared to remain calm and focused? What would be different?

Day Seven: Today spend 15 minutes reflecting and journaling about what you have learned this week and what you value about your practice of deep breathing and mindfulness.

As a reward for using your "mental floss" in doing this weeks work, you get to read the next chapter which teaches the use of mindfulness in eating a piece of.......

'CHOCOLATE'

"And the day came when the risk it took to remain tightly closed in a bud was more painful than the risk it took to bloom."

—Anais Nin

18. Practice mindfulness as you eat chocolate!

Here is a practical and fun way to experience and practice mindfulness. Let's use the wonderful tool of chocolate and let's get right to it. The first thing you do is purchase a bag of foil wrapped chocolate kisses. If you are allergic to chocolate or have a medical condition that suggests that you should not eat chocolate, this exercise works just as well using a bag of raisins The purpose of this exercise is to engage mindfully in an activity that we normally do mindlessly. Most people unwrap the chocolate, pop it in their mouths, chew a few times, swallow, and reach for the next piece without even thinking about the delicious treat they have just consumed. Often they find themselves with nothing more than an empty bag, lots of little silver papers and a a big bundle of guilt. We would like to suggest another way, the way of mindfulness as you eat chocolate. It slows the process down, engages you fully in the present moment and shows you how to focus. It enhances a simply delicious experience. During this practice, make note of how much more enjoyable it is to eat a piece of chocolate mindfully as compared to how you used to eat a chocolate kiss. Enjoy.

Begin by placing one piece of chocolate in a cup and proceed to a quiet private place where you won't be disturbed for about 15 minutes. When you are settled in a chair, begin by becoming aware of your breathing. Use the techniques that you have practiced in the last chapter to bring your breath and mind into the present moment. Take some deep breaths and become relaxed and comfortable. Begin to think about the piece of chocolate. Spend a few seconds looking at it and imagining how it will feel and taste in your mouth. Next, pick up the piece of chocolate but do not take off the silver foil. Hold it between your thumb and index finger and begin smelling the chocolate and noticing its shape. Do this for 15 seconds. Stay in the present moment. Do not allow yourself to be distracted. Now slowly unwrap the chocolate and experience what it smells like now that it is unwrapped. Bring the chocolate to your lips and slowly rub it on the outside of your lips and see what it feels like. Keep your awareness focused on what you are experiencing in the present moment. You may feel a little silly but note this feeling and let it pass. Continue by gently placing the chocolate on your tongue but do not bite or chew it. Let it sit there in your mouth as it begins to melt on its own. Take notice of how it feels and tastes. Wait for the chocolate to melt completely. Stay in the present moment experiencing the true essence of a piece of chocolate like you have never experienced it before. Notice the taste, the sweetness and the texture of the chocolate. When the chocolate is completely melted get your journal and begin working on the daily practices. Write a few paragraphs in your journal about practicing mindfulness while eating a piece of chocolate.

Daily Practices

Day One: Write a few paragraphs in your journal about practicing mindfulness while eating a piece of chocolate. Visualize how this experience can help you practice mindfulness in other situations. Write a few examples of how you might apply the above lesson to other circumstances.

Day Two: Slow down and become mindful of your daily rituals such as washing dishes, cleaning vegetables, brushing teeth, shaving, combing the hair of a child, making love. Choose one or two daily tasks that you will focus on during the coming week where you can apply this practice to gain deeper awareness of the value of mindfulness in your life.

Days Three, Four, Five, and Six: Take 15 minutes each day to write in your journal about the experiences you are having as you begin to slow down and live your life more mindfully, focusing on the present moment and paying attention to the essence of your daily life.

Day Seven: Take 15 minutes to journal about how the awareness of your practice of mindfulness is helping you to wake up in your life, to know and to understand the value of living in the present moment.

BON APPETITE FOR LIFE!

19. Take "5"

"There is more to life than increasing its speed."

—Gandhi

I have heard it said that it is not the notes that make music; it is the pauses between the notes. I believe that this is true for our life. Modern life often occurs at such a rapid pace that we are always quickly moving on to what is next. This not only takes its toll on our physical health, but also on the quality of relationships and overall experiences. Life at a rapid pace is a superficial life. Meaning is created and experienced in the moments of silence.

Become more aware of your natural rhythms of energy and attention. Connect with the ebb and flow. Step out of the feeling that there is just too much going on and the feelings of powerlessness to change this.

Taking moments of quiet reflection allows you to more fully experience life and to ultimately identify just what you want for your life, relationships and experiences. This practice of slowing down your pace and practicing the art of doing nothing is a difficult one to comprehend. It can be even harder to implement. Collectively we tend to be uncomfortable "doing nothing". It feels wrong to many of us. It activates an internal pressure and feeling that we need to be doing something. We often feel the need to fill our time and be more productive.

Give yourself permission to do nothing. Give yourself permission to slow down the pace of your life. Give yourself permission to embrace silence. Taking moments of quite reflection will allow you to more fully experience your own life. Taking moments of quite reflection allows us to transcend useless repetitive circles of thoughts that allow creativities thoughts to emerge. Start with quietly contemplating Carl Sandburg's words: "One of the greatest necessities in America is to discover creative solitude" or the words of Blaise Pascal; "All man's miseries derive from not being able to sit quietly in a room alone".

Some of us are either going too fast or too slow. Some of us have difficulty striking the right balance. My own tendency, like that of many super achievers, is to go too fast. I am learning to give myself the gift of rest, relaxation and recharge time.

Many super achievers discount the value of rest, seeing it as wasteful or being unproductive. Rest includes getting enough sleep at night, taking breaks, silent time or just laying down quietly. Rest, paradoxically, might be the most important 'activity' that we do. Physical and mental renewal makes people more productive and makes activities more pleasurable.

The practices this week will emphasize how giving yourself the gift of down time can help you recharge yourself physically, emotionally and spiritually.

Daily Practices

Day One: Allow yourself to enjoy simply BEING. Be alone with yourself without any of the common props (newspaper, book, TV, radio, etc...) for at least 15 minutes.

Day Two: Focus on slowing down your pace. Maintain a healthy breathing rhythm.

Day Three: Gain perspective by temporarily pulling back. It is important to be focused, yet it is also important to untangle from being intensely focused. This can connect you with where you lost your vision and help you be more selective about where you are putting your efforts.

Day Four: Get out your daily planner. Schedule gaps into your day. This can help you learn to savor each moment. It will also allow you to more fully digest impressions. Keep your perspective fresh.

Day Five: Remember, relapse is part of recovery. If you are trying to be a recovering over achiever, you will likely have relapses. Slow down enough to pay attention to your thoughts, your emotions, your body, and your energy. A large percentage of wisdom flows out of being more patient, flexible, and creative. These experiences are more likely to be PRESENT if you are.

Day Six: Remember we all get the same amount of time each day. Learn to treat time as your friend. Cooperate with the natural flow of time and energy. Identify when your energy tends to be at a high point and when it is at a low point. How long can you work without a break. How can you best maximize your cycles of energy? How can you best make use of your breaks?

Day Seven: Build in quiet times to ease transitions. Close your eyes for 5 minutes before you leave work at the end of the day. Stop at a park near home to sit quietly before you go home. Identify times you could build in quite times to ease transitions.

Dr. Mike Davison, Kay Guzder

20. Don't just do something, sit there

"No thought, no action, no movement, total stillness: only thus can one manifest the true nature and law of things from within and unconsciously, and at last become one with heaven and earth."

—Lao Taz

We need quite time built into our day so we can just be with our thoughts. I am not talking about day dreaming or having grand fantasies. I am suggesting just having time each day without a newspaper, television, radio, conversation or any other things that may drown out our connection to yourself. I am not suggesting that you go off to an ashram in India or live in solitude, more simply, carve out a small space everyday to sit quietly all by yourself.

For some this quiet time may take the form of a formal mediation practice. However, it can simply be a walk, taking a long bath, or any other ritual that may allow you to connect more fully with yourself and bring down the pace that many of us live in.

How you make use of this time may change over time, or

you may have a variety of quite time rituals. This important ritual allows you to stop, reflect, notice and enjoy who you are. Allow yourself to reflect on the past, present, future or nothing specific. I have implemented this process of daily renewal and rejuvenation in my own life and it has increased my feelings of well being and tranquility. I often use this quite time ritual as a transition between activities or roles that I need to play in my life. For example, stopping at a park on the way home from work to have 10 minutes of quite times helps me feel cleared, centered, energized and ready to be more fully engaged at home as a husband and a father.

I believe that just as physical exercise strengthens the body, quite time strengthens the spirit. For me it allows space to reflect on my existence and my life's purpose. Being more connected to my essence allows me to more effectively prioritize and deal with any challenges that inevitably come up in life.

This week remember that slowing down helps you look at things from a new point of view. When you even slightly shift your perspective about yourself, others or the world around you, changes in your feelings and behavior will naturally and gently follow suit. Your life really can be less of a struggle and more joyful when you learn to be more fully present in the moment. Being more fully present in everything you do is the golden key to personal peace. The practices this week will help you train yourself to be more fully present and more fully alive.

Daily Practices

Day One: Walk slowly and gently let your attention come to rest on the tactile sensations throughout your body. Just notice the sensations in your body and how they are related to the environment. This is a simple 'grounding' exercise. I know it sounds simple, however, reading about it will not have the same impact as doing it.

Day Two: This practice you can do sitting, lying, walking or standing. Simply and gently focus your attention on your senses, especially vision and hearing, and observe colors and sounds. Focus on the sensory experiences as opposed to emotional reactions or logical conclusions related to your sensory experiences. This exercise can help any agitation melt away as you can embrace the serenity of simply being present.

Day Three: Simply sit and gently gaze into the space in front of you. Just allow your mind to relax. Simply let your attention settle on the awareness of being aware. As strange as it sounds, in this exercise you really do nothing. You just know that you are aware, and settle your attention in that knowing, with no other objective. This practice helps you become aware of the nature of your consciousness. Why do this? Because you will discover a stillness that is innate to our awareness. This exercise helps you cultivate the natural vividness of experience and can greatly enhance self-awareness and self-knowledge.

Day Four: I conducted research with a colleague and friend that involved collecting several thousand antidotes regarding individual's cocaine cravings early in their recovery from cocaine addiction. We found that cocaine urges or cravings, which are not acted upon (or merely observed), lasted on average for 3 minutes. We can put up with anything for 3 minutes, especially if we know that experience is always in flux. This research also helped us see that anything that is 'fought' is given more energy and prolongs the negative experience. Think of how this applies to your own emotions or experiences of being overwhelmed. Think about a specific past experience and how trying to "fight off" an overwhelming emotion or experience actually prolonged your distress. Think about how simply being still and silent will allow you to stay more connected to your true essence—peace.

Day Five: Today practice this exercise from Jon Kabat-Zinn's work that can help you 'try out' the concept of mindfulness in your own life.

When in a situation that makes you angry or upset, or just annoyed, try watching your reactions. Try to experience mindfulness as a pot into which you can put all your feelings and just be with them and let them slowly cook. You don't have to do anything with your emotions right away. They will become more cooked, more easily digested just by holding them in this pot of mindfulness.

Observe the way your feelings are created by your mind's view of things. Maybe this view is not complete (or maybe it is). If you can be courageous enough to explore putting strong emotions into the pot and just holding them and letting them cook, you may come to know yourself in new ways and free yourself of some old, limiting views.

Day Six: Playfully experiment with slowing down and being more fully present in your life. Try at least one of the following "experiments" today. 1) Schedule in a chunk of time every day to do NOTHING. 2). Drive 10 miles under the speed limit for an entire day (If you already do—drive the speed limit for an entire day). 3). When you eat—only eat. Don't watch TV or engage in other activities. 4). Let the phone ring at least 3 times before you answer it. 5). Have slower conversations. Listen more (Don't formulate responses when someone else is speaking).

Day Seven: Identify other ways to playfully alter your pace, your routines and your automatic patterns of thinking, feeling, behaving, and relating. Implement at least one of them for the entire day. Use your journal to write about your experience(s).

21. Finding peace in nature: "Meet the crazy lady who hugs trees"

"To be rooted is perhaps the most important and least recognized need of the human soul."

—Simone Weil, French Philosopher

I have always loved trees. When I was a child I would lie on the ground watching the sunlight filter through the leaves and imagine I was in heaven. I loved to climb trees, sit in their branches, watch the birds build nests, and wonder what it would be like to be able to fly. As an adult my love of trees hasn't diminished, if anything it has grown and as I visit different parts of the country I take particular notice of the trees.

At Peninsula State Park in Wisconsin there are majestic towering grandfather fir trees that watch over the young sapling grandchildren growing at their feet. The deep green color of the fir branches blend beautifully with the white birch trees so abundant in the area and together they present a breathtaking landscape. I find such peace and serenity in the forest and always want to share the magic with others. I've had several of what I like to call "my tree experiences", but the one I will always remember as my favorite happened in the woods of Wisconsin. I was visiting a park and decided to take a walk along a path that encircled the lake. About two miles into my walk I came around a corner and saw the most magnificent tree ever. The trunk was so huge it took up almost all of the walking space on the path and crowded the rustic old boy scout cabins lining the shore. The rest of the trunk roots grew down to the waters edge and into the lake. The canopy covered several of the outlying cabins and completely embraced the area. I guessed that this tree must have been growing here for hundreds of years. I was pulled to the tree like a magnet and following my impulse, never hesitated, as I moved in and hugged it. I held on tight and turned my face so I could press closer to the tree trunk. I lost track of time and place and became totally unaware of anyone around me. To this day I have no idea if anyone was watching me spontaneously embrace and experience this gift of nature. Suddenly I had no inhibitions; I didn't care if I looked silly or crazy. I was so concentrated on being in the present moment that I was able to fully experience a deep and abiding connection with one of nature's most beautiful creations. Since then I have been known to tie pretty pastel ribbons to some tree branches in my yard in the springtime, celebrate birthdays by tying ribbons to my friend's tree branches and place candles in vases underneath the trees at twilight and watch them glow under the branches in front of my window.

If you haven't learned the lessons of the trees yet, why not go out and look for the trees that call to you. Visit with them. Learn what they have to teach. You might hear them telling you to take advantage of what is available to you. Reach high. Nourish your roots. Branch out and breathe in the air deeply. Partake of water and nutrients. Remain steadfast in times of adversity. Be a source of solace and extend yourself to others in need. Believe in your own beauty. Recognize you are a creation of God and in so being know you have the capacity to create peace and harmony.

Once you learn the lessons of the trees, don't forget to try new ideas. In the spring, stand under a flowering apple or cherry tree and let the petals rain down all over and around you. In the summer find your favorite tree and sit beneath it with a cool drink. Lean your back against the trunk and read a book. When fall comes and you see the brilliant colors, take time to listen to the rustle of the leaves in the wind. Think about the ebb and flow of life and examine how well you are living yours. In the winter when it seems the trees are asleep and the leaves have all died, take some snapshots of the lacy branches and the infrastructure that is not seen when trees are in full bloom. Let them remind you that, like trees, we have inner strength and the capacity to persevere and blossom forth again and again. While on the journey of your personal path to peace, the lessons of the trees.

Daily Practices

Day One: Spend some time reflecting on the lessons of the trees.

Day Two: Spend some time thinking and journaling about ways you can recapture the sense of wonder, playfulness and freedom that you felt as a child.

Day Three: Spend 15 minutes journaling about how you place roadblocks in your way that keep you stifled, self conscious and robbed of spontaneity.

Dr. Mike Davison, Kay Guzder

Day Four: Spend some time journaling about what compels you to embrace your inhibitions. Ask yourself what is stopping you from experiencing and accomplishing what you want in life? Write about the fears and inhibitions that prevent you from enjoying the simple pleasures that surround you every day.

Day Five: Spend some time answering the following questions in your journal: Are you afraid of looking foolish? Are you afraid of being criticized? Are you afraid of looking like a failure? Are you afraid of failing at something you really want to try? Are you afraid of trying and succeeding? What do you want to be doing different five years from now considering that you know you have the power to make choices and changes in your life?

Day Six: Spend some time reflecting and journaling about how you can begin to incorporate the changes you want to make in your life. Choose the issues you want to work on and write a mission statement. Answering the following questions: How have you thought about these issues in the past? How are you thinking about them now? How do you want to bring about change in the future? How and when will you begin to make these changes? Be specific when you write your plan of action. Include simple actions you can begin working on this week.

Day Seven: Today take time to rest and have some recreation. Remember that the base word in recreation is the word recreate. It is through recreation that we recreate our energy and vitality. We awaken our senses and sharpen our ability to think creatively. Take the time to visit and thank a special tree, one that you can revisit on a regular basis to get refreshed and replenished. Recapture your sense of playfulness and feel the freedom of spontaneity.

22. "Soul food served here": Nurturing yourself using relaxation and meditation

"Treasure your physical being as a vehicle that choruses your soul. Once you have the inner way, the outer way will follow".

—Dr. Wayne Dyer

While driving through the countryside one day my attention was drawn to an aging yellowed signboard in a small country churchyard. It read *"Soul Food Served Here"*. I might have passed by quite unaware of the gift the universe was offering had it not been for that clever little sign. It made me stop and think about the simple ways in which we can nurture our souls by taking a bit of time here and there to replenish ourselves. The message on that little signboard speaks to us of our soul's need for daily nourishment.

One way you can care for yourself is by taking the time to identify what you hunger for. Ask yourself what is it that needs attention? What needs to be put back into your life or perhaps brought into it for the first time? What will give you a feeling of satisfaction, peacefulness and hope? What needs to be incorporated in your life to relieve your busy mind so you can create a space to become aware of your thoughts and needs, as well as your hopes and dreams?

When we travel by plane we know the pilot is guided by instruments that lead the plane toward its destination. It may be surprising to learn that even when on automatic pilot the plane is not flying directly on course. The automatic pilot is continuously directed by computers to make corrections to keep the plane on course. Likewise, you may find you can benefit from listening to your inner guidance system as you travel along life's path. Your inner guidance system corrects and keeps you on course moving toward a more personally fulfilling lifestyle.

A tried and true first step to getting in tune with your personal guidance system is to develop a practice of meditation. Meditative practice harnesses and directs energy away from distractions and negative thinking. The practice of relaxation helps you become less anxious and cope more effectively with ongoing stress. The goal is to create and enjoy a more peaceful lifestyle. By making these practices part of your daily ritual, you will be able to formulate new ideas and find solutions to problems that have kept you preoccupied and robbed of energy. A willingness to focus your mind on peaceful, loving, supportive, and constructive ideas is all that is needed to start a practice of meditation and relaxation. Use the following technique to bring yourself to a place of awareness and begin to identify what you want to choose from the menu life offers you. Decide to give yourself some "soul food".

Find a quiet place where you won't be interrupted. Turn off the TV, radio, and telephone and let the people around you know you are going to be unavailable for the next ten to fifteen minutes. This is about the amount of time it takes to shower so it shouldn't be difficult to claim some personal time for yourself. When you are seated comfortably in a chair close your eyes and bring your thoughts to your heart center. This is the area in the middle of your chest where your heart resides. With mind focused on your heart center, begin to visualize the beating of your heart. Anytime during this relaxation technique you find your mind wandering, just return your thoughts to the simple visualization of your beating heart. Now take three deep breaths inhaling through your nose and exhaling through your mouth. Slowly count one, two, three, four, five, as you inhale and again as you exhale. Become aware if you are holding a lot of tension in your neck and shoulder muscles. Many people feel tightness in these areas. This is where the stress is manifesting physically. It is important to concentrate on the breathing as a way of letting go of the tightness. Relax your neck and shoulders and let gravity pull the shoulders down and away from the neck area. If your shoulders are hunched up in tension, move them down naturally by letting your arms fall limply to your sides. If there is tightness in the back of the neck, let the stress go and loosen up in this area as well. Experience this released and relaxed feeling for a few moments before you continue. When you are ready, begin to visualize your nostrils as you take in life giving breaths to fill your lungs. Become aware of the cool temperature of the oxygen as you inhale and exhale several time through your nostrils. As you concentrate on breathing bring your attention to the cool air moving through your left nostril. Try to focus only on the left nostril as you inhale and exhale five times. After you become aware, comfortable and relaxed with your breathing meditation through the left nostril, begin to visualize your right nostril and repeat the process focusing on the cool air flowing in and out of your right nostril. After completing the right nostril breathing meditation bring your focus back to breathing through both nostrils simultaneously. When you have completed the nostril breathing meditation sit for a while becoming aware of the deep feeling of relaxation you have created for yourself. When you are ready open your eyes and sit still for a few minutes more to gain your balance and become fully alert. Take note of how relaxed you feel. Notice the sense of clarity you have after completing this exercise.

By participating in this exercise you are practicing a form of self hypnosis. By relaxing your muscles and redirecting your thought process you help to lower your stress level and release the tension in your body. Think about how you will find time to incorporate this relaxation technique into your daily life to nourish your mind, body, and spirit.

Daily Practices

Day One: Spend some time reviewing and practicing the relaxation exercise.

Day Two: Repeat the relaxation exercise and journal about what came to your attention as you proceeded through the meditation. Particularly note any positive or negative thoughts you experienced during the exercise.

Day Three: Repeat the relaxation exercise and journal any ideas about what future benefits you hope to gain as you continue to develop your daily practice. What do you want to bring into your life? What do you want to change?

Day Four: Repeat the relaxation exercise. Become aware of what thoughts go through your mind as you sit quietly relaxed in your chair. Spend some time journaling your thoughts. Are there any problems you want to solve so you can get on with your life in a peaceful nurturing way?

Day Five: Practice the relaxation exercise today and notice if you are able to achieve a relaxed meditative state sooner than in the first few times you practiced. Are you able to think more clearly after the breathing and relaxing exercise? Journal any thoughts you have about your personal practice.

Day Six: Practice the relaxation and meditation exercise and journal any modifications you wish to make to your routine. Personalize your experience to meet your particular needs. Modify as needed and make notes in your journal about any changes you wish to make.

Day Seven: Spend some time practicing your relaxation technique and then write a few paragraphs in your journal describing your experience of participating in this practice throughout the week. Write about how you can utilize breathing relaxation meditation as your personal guidance system. What needs attention? What do you hunger for? What do you want to choose from the menu life has to offer?

Section IV. Attitudes & Actions that Further Cultivate Personal Peace

23. Willingness

"Not knowing when the dawn will come, I open every door".

—Emily Dickinson

"You can't make me do it, so there!" When I was a kid I would shout this statement at other kids to declare my power and defend my territory on the playground. If the encounter involved my parents or teachers, I was usually less brave and confrontational but I would still say the words under my breath. Adolescence brought about new tactics. I learned to be less openly defensive but held on to a stubborn streak and my willfulness didn't serve me well. Too much emotional energy was spent digging in my heels. Anger and frustration became entrenched and negative emotions were driving my existence. I missed a lot of opportunities for fun and growth because I was blinded by my stubborn attitude. It took a long time for me to see that I was only hurting myself by being so closed minded. I engaged in a personal war filled with unnecessary battles. Today the old quote "I wish I would have known then what I know now," resonates for me. Life would have been much smoother had I followed a gentler path. But like most people I had to learn the hard way, through trial and error, until I matured enough to realize that I needed to find better coping skills to meet life's challenges. I had to be willing to change my old way of thinking in order to learn and grow. I had to let go of my fears and defensiveness to be able to take advantage of opportunities that would lead me to a more satisfying existence.

Eventually my path led me to graduate studies in psychology. It was there that I learned that many negative emotions are fear based and that people keep their fears deeply hidden. They use different defenses to protect themselves I learned that some fears don't get expressed as willfulness or stubbornness like mine did. They are acted out in different, but equally troublesome, ways. Some people find themselves stuck in people pleasing roles. They seek the approval of others. Some are afraid of making mistakes. Some are afraid of rejection. Feeling of inadequacy keep some folks feeling stuck and afraid so they resist change. Many people remain in dysfunctional relationships that involve physical or emotional abuse. Their lives are filled with the heaviness of inertia, frustration and unhappiness. Some people sit back and let others make their choices rather than take the initiative to change. Many of us stay hidden behind our fears and let life pass us by. Then we wonder why we feel sad, disappointed, frustrated and depressed. That's how it was for me for much of my youth. I was the poster child of the rebellious teenager, modeling the picture of willfulness. I was sad, confused and stuck.

Willfulness as described in the dictionary is, "governed by will without regard to reason" In contrast the word *willingness* is described as "inclined or favorably disposed in mind, ready to go, accepted voluntarily without reluctance, wish or desire, often combined with determination to reach something desired." At some point, most of us recognize we need to compromise our wills if we're to bring about change in our lives. Sooner or later we all get dissatisfied with the dysfunctional coping mechanisms we are using to hide our fears, frustrations and perceived inadequacies. These obstacles help us recognize that change is desirable and necessary. After repeatedly bumping our heads against these obstacles we realize that something is not working well for us. This is when we have our best chance for change, we become willing to take a fresh look and begin lowering our defenses. Unfortunately, change is not easy and frequently we begin to make excuses for avoiding the steps we know we need to take. We get distracted and stuck in the old familiar ways. Are you one of those "yes, but" people that tell yourself you want to change and then immediately make excuses that dispute your good ideas and intentions. Do you tell yourself, "I'll wait until after the kids grow up," or "after I save more money," or "I'll be ready after I lose weight," or "after I retire," or, "I just don't think I can do it"? Do you recognize yourself in these examples? What is your excuse? Are you recycling old mental or emotional tapes that keep you in 'the rocking chair position"? You rock forward and back, but always end up stuck in the same old place.

If you recognize yourself in any of these statements it's time to get down to some good old fashioned soul searching. Time to ask yourself some hard questions, the ones where we hold up the mirror, look ourselves in the eye and ask if we are being truthful or conning ourselves to avoid change? Is it that *we can't* make the changes or that we are *not willing* to change? Ask yourself if old fears are interfering with your decision to move in the direction you desire? Are you ready to examine your capacity to participate willingly and move ahead courageously?

If you can be authentic and truthful in answering these

questions you will have a better chance of identifying the obstacles that are blocking your way. The answers can help you break out of old patterns of thinking that have kept you stuck. A new approach will help you to circumvent the old "start, stop and fail" routine that fills you with negative emotions. Open your heart to willingness and let your inner voice lead you to your personal wisdom, a wisdom that will guide you. Write about your obstacles and struggles as you try to break old habits and patterns. By writing you slow down the thoughts that slip through your mind quickly. If you concretize your thoughts in writing you will be able to recognize you obstacles and mistakes. Then you will begin to recognize how to proceed more towards change. If you can be truthful, thoughtful and reflective, your inner wisdom will help you move toward the life changes you desire. Think in terms of positive sentences that begin with words such as, "I will be… I want to be… I used to be… I let go of… I remember when I used to…I now am…" Have the courage to ask yourself the hard questions and try to answer as honestly as you can: Are you willing to seriously commit to the changes you desire? What is standing in your way? Is it stubbornness, is it fear? Identify the obstacles and then put on your problem solving hat. Break the challenges down into smaller manageable parts. Wrap your heart around your ideas and see how far your own wisdom will take you when you are fueled by willingness. Don't let opportunities slip by year after year. Think about what makes you feel fulfilled. What makes you feel good? What makes you smile? What fills your heart with love and passion? Focus on the possibilities and opportunities that life offers instead of the obstacles and setbacks and you will be closer to realizing your dreams. You won't become discouraged if you remember this formula for success: make small changes over time with a willing attitude and spirit. Believe your inner wisdom.

Dr. Mike Davison, Kay Guzder

Daily Practices

Day One: Spend 15 minutes writing in your journal about your tendency to be stubborn and willful. If you do not identify with being stubborn or willful, write about an obstacle that has kept you from making the changes you want in your life.

Day Two: Reflect on the phrase "I wish I knew then what I know now" and journal about an experience in your life when you found the wisdom and maturity to make positive shifts toward change.

Day Three: Identify one change you want to make in your life. Write a paragraph about how you will benefit by making this change.

Day Four: Identify the obstacles you think you will face when you begin to make the changes you desire. Ask yourself what are your internal obstacles? What are the external obstacles you need to overcome? Write a few paragraphs in your journal answering the above questions.

Day Five: Think about the excuses you make to avoid taking action toward the changes you desire. Write these excuses in your journal. Ask yourself how these excuses are affecting your life. Are the excuses keeping you stuck and spinning your wheels? Are they preventing you from taking the necessary steps needed to move toward your goals?

Day Six: Create a plan of action in your journal. List the steps you need to take to implement the changes you desire.

Day Seven: Write a few paragraphs in your journal about the concept of willingness. Write about your willingness to face the obstacles you've identified. Rate your level of willingness to commit to your goal on a scale of 1 to 10 where 1 is "I am not willing" and 10 is "nothing on earth could stop me, I'm totally committed to this change." Write a few paragraphs about another time in your life when you overcame your fears and challenged yourself to find your wisdom and courage to bring about positive change. Journal about how you can apply the same internal strength and wisdom to your present situation.

24. Laughing all the way

"If we couldn't laugh, we would all go insane".

—Jimmy Buffet

As it has been said, "laughter is the best medicine". While this is a bit of a cliché, it has a great deal of scientific validation behind it. A consciousness of joy and humor fosters personal peace.

Laughter fosters a sense of confidence and emotional and physical wellbeing. It's amazing how people gather around a person who exudes confidence, laughter and joy.

Think about it. How many "successful" people do you know who have gloom and doom personalities? If a person like that even exists, it's likely any success that comes to them is out of pure chance. They certainly don't have the personal peace that allows them to enjoy any material success.

True successes are people who have developed the ability to smile in the face of challenge and who step right in and take charge when others just stand around doing nothing. And they keep going when others give up. The confident person hears obstacles say, "Jump over me" not, "Too bad, now you'll never make it." They are willing to do what they need to do to succeed.

To really develop a magnetic personality, start working on a cheerful attitude. You can not start too early. Actually, if you learn the power of cheerfulness and self-confidence, it will attract the right people and the right circumstances.

The importance of enthusiasm and a good sense of humor can not be overstated at this point. Whenever you lose your ability to laugh, your physical and emotional health start to decline rapidly.

Don't you enjoy being around someone with a genuine laugh and fun sense of humor? It really is one of the characteristics of great personalities, that capacity to take things lightly.

So laugh heartily! A real laugh springs naturally out of confidence and a positive mental attitude. Never miss a chance to laugh aloud. A smile and a good chuckle will encourage —but out and out laughter is the real thing that will draw others to you. They will wonder who on earth is enjoying life that much!!

You can triumph over challenges and obstacles in life when you believe and stay excited about your life! People are drawn to the confident person who is motivated, passionate, and exude joy.

Choose enthusiasm and an attitude of joy, and you'll find yourself winning again and again. Choose to find the humor in any situation. Choose to take your mission seriously but yourself lightly. After all, you know why angels can fly, don't you? They take themselves lightly.

Daily Practices

Day One: Identify in your journal what makes you laugh. Build you own humor library.

Day Two: Identify in your journal people you know that are funny. Surround yourself with funny people—be with them every chance you get.

Day Three: Make a commitment to use humor for positive, playful, uplifting, healing and loving purposes throughout the day.

Day Four: Be on alert for the jokes and absurdities you encounter. Write them down. Share your observations with your friends and family.

Day Five: Today go to the public library and check out one humorous book and/or one humorous movie.

Day Six: Read for at least 20 minutes from a humorous book. Observe and document the emotional and physical impact that laughter has on you.

Day Seven: Watch one of your favorite comedy movies. Make a note on the impact that the humor, joy and laughter had on you.

25. Finding humor in everyday life, or "The day my barbeque grill went up John Jackson's hill!"

I had the good fortune to live in Tennessee for a few years and one of the most important lessons I learned from the Native Tennesseans is that humor can be found everywhere, any time and it is yours for the taking if you just keep your eyes and ears open. Humor is a great healer, a natural stress buster and a sure cure for all of the "gets me mad, gets me down, gets on my nerves" situations that show up regularly in our daily lives. Some Tennesseans save up stories for a whole year before attending the annual "Storytellers, Fiddlers Convention and Mule Day Celebration." They do their best to tell the most outrageous hilarious stories you've ever heard and get people to believe them. What I learned from that special time living in Tennessee is to keep my eyes and ears open, look for the bright and funny side of life and save up my stories. You never know when you'll get to tell one that will help somebody get a break from what's got them down. In the process you might even help yourself pull

Dr. Mike Davison, Kay Guzder

out of the doldrums. To prove my point I'll tell you a story that happened to me and I'll swear to it!

Shortly after moving to Tennessee, my family adopted a golden retriever puppy and we wanted to give her a Tennessee name. I wandered into a little country store and saw a sign prominently displaying their daily special, a big cool tray of delicious looking dessert labeled "Nanner Puddin". I tried some, found it tasted just like banana pudding and decided this was a fitting name for my sweet little golden Tennessee puppy. As time went by and the puppy grew, I had a pretty big Tennessee girl on my hands and she was showing a strong genetic throwback to some bygone rodeo days. When I tried to teach her to fetch the morning paper, she went into my neighbor's yard and retrieved their paper, proceeding to run around the yard shaking it to shreds. This meant I had to retrieve Nanner and give the neighbor my paper. As a result of the early morning antics I decided it was time for "Dogzilla" to spend some time in our backyard tethered to the barbeque grill. We hadn't yet fenced our two acre property and I needed a few minutes peace to make some phone calls. Our barbeque grill was no wimpy small time grill. This was the deluxe model mounted on a sturdy stand with whitewall tires. It was big, heavy, and meant for some serious barbequing. By now "Nan", as we affectionately called her, was no wimp either. She was tipping the scales at about 85 lbs and could take down a goat if the opportunity presented itself. Our home was situated on one of the few flat areas in the neighborhood and sat at the bottom of a formidable hill. Our next door neighbor's property was defined by a sharp uphill grade and every home thereafter sat on a steeper incline. Our property was not only flat but had few shade trees and only scruffy bits of scrub grass. We had ordered a truckload of dirt to be delivered to the backyard so we could begin to grow some grass. I was on the phone chatting away with my friend when I became aware of the delivery truck backing into our driveway toward the rear of the house. I could hear the long distinctive tell-tale beeps and the whirr of the gears as the dump truck began to dump its load. Next I heard an unmistakable thud as the dirt was dropped and then a thunderous clang as the trapdoor rejoined the back of the dump truck. Still on the phone, I stood looking toward the backyard through the narrow windows of the family room French doors. I was about to remark to my friend that I had to hang up because the truck had just delivered the dirt to the backyard when I stopped mid-sentence and uttered incredulously, "Maria, my barbeque grill just went up John Jackson's Hill." All I could see through those narrow windows was my grill beating it up the hill tipped up on two wheels with utensils flying out from the sides. I dropped the phone, ran outside and up the hill, and caught up with my bedraggled Golden Retriever still trying to pull the grill higher and farther away from the dreaded dump truck. She had met her match and hauled that grill farther and faster than anyone ever dreamed possible.

Our Nan became a legend in the neighborhood and her fame lives on to this day. She is famous for creating the challenge that became an annual block party event every year thereafter. The only change is that now it's not the neighborhood dogs that haul the grills up John Jackson's hill, it's the neighborhood Dads flexing their muscles and vying for first place to prove they can match Nan's speed and stamina. The contest is widely known as the annual "John Jackson's Hill Barbeque Grill Pull" and is followed by the "Old Fool's Annual Riding Lawnmower Derby down John Jackson's Hill"!!!

Look inside and outside yourself for opportunities to bring a good belly laugh to your life and to the lives of others.

Humor is infectious. It helps you get through the tough times and lightens the burden. Actively look for humor in everyday life. It's all around you I'm going to close this chapter with a poem I recently saw in a major department store catalogue. This little ditty is advertised as, "Inscribed on a tile and ready to display on a lovely pewter easel." It reads as follows:

"May the light always find you on a dreary day,
When you need to be home, may you find your way.
May you always have courage to take a chance,
And never find frogs in your underpants."

—*Penned by an anonymous "Middle Aged Scandinavian".*

Daily Practices

Day One: Spend some time reflecting on the concept of humor as a healing tool.

Day Two: Journal about whether you deflect or invite humor into your life.

Day Three: Write a few paragraphs about some funny incidents that happened to you. Tell them to some of your friends and ask them to relate their funniest personal experiences to you.

Day Four: Write about your reaction to yesterday's assignment. Did you find it difficult? Was it intimidating to tell your stories to your friends? If this was a negative experience for you, you might want to check your internal monitor to see if you need to get reacquainted with your sense of humor. While you're at it, check to make sure you still have the capacity to connect to your friends using humor as a healing tool.

Day Five: Stretch yourself today by making it your goal to make someone have a good laugh.

Day Six: Write a few paragraphs about yesterday's assignment. Were you able to recognize the abundance of humorous situations you can relate to others? Did you recognize the benefits to yourself when you connected to another through the use of humor?

Day Seven: Remind yourself today how good it feels to be alive and have laughter in your life and to share it with others. Make a plan to incorporate humor into your life and use it as a tool for healing. Laughter is a freedom which resides in our hearts and minds, you need only keep your eyes and ears open. Contemplate on the places in the world where people have little reason to laugh but nonetheless they do. Don't underestimate the power of humor to heal.

26. Thank you, thank you, thank you

"Let us rise up and be thankful, for if we didn't learn a lot today, at least we learned a little, and if we didn't learn a little, at least we didn't get sick, and if we got sick, at least we didn't die; so, let us all be thankful".

—Buddha

Things don't always go the way we want them to. Life inevitably has its ups and downs. Challenges come my way from time-to-time. I have not yet figured out a way to live an effortless and problem free life. However, I have taped into the next best thing. The next best thing for me is living in gratitude. To quote the popular saying, have an "Attitude of gratitude". The greatest prayer we can pray is one of deep gratitude.

In my work as a Clinical Psychologist, I have seen many depressed individuals over the years. While I am not suggesting this is a complete conceptualization of depression, but folks who are depressed have difficulty accessing feelings of gratitude. This perspective is biased toward all that is wrong and all they do not have. This does not mean that depressed people are making up "negative" things, but I am suggesting that they are likely to filter out that which they can be grateful for. I am not exactly suggesting positive thinking. I am suggesting more of what I call inclusive thinking. That is acknowledging it all, the good, the bad, and the ugly.

There is always something to be grateful for. It may be things. People. Health. A stable job. The list goes on and on. Remember, I am not suggesting that you deny the challenges. However, don't deny the "good stuff" either.

I believe that having a deep spirit of gratitude is contagious. It somehow seems to give others permission to stop and take notice for that which they can be grateful for. Look for opportunities to cultivate gratitude. Keep a gratitude journal. Say prayers of gratitude. Write a letter of thanks to someone who has positively impacted you. Don't miss an opportunity to say words of appreciation and gratitude to people in your life.

While the idea of expressing gratitude or keeping a gratitude journal may seem overly simplistic, I must tell you—it works! I also know that individuals who have kept a gratitude journal for as brief as 6 weeks have been studied and have been shown to have a greater sense of subjective well-being and also had increases in immune system function.

Daily Practices

Day One: Read this beautiful prayer from Marianne Williamson that amplifies the importance of gratitude and being clear about what impact you want to have on the world, and write your reflections in your journal.

A New Day

Dear God,

Thank you for this new day, its beauty and its light.
Thank you for my chance to begin again.
Free me from the limitations of yesterday.
Today I am reborn.
May I become more fully a reflection of your radiance?
Give me strength and compassion and courage and wisdom.
Show me the light in others and myself.
May I recognize the good that is available everywhere.
May I be, this day, an instrument of love and healing.
Lead me into gentle pastures.
Give me deep peace that I might serve you most deeply.

Amen.

Day Two: Take at least 10 minutes to close your eyes, quiet yourself and recollect experiences over the past several months when people were kind to you, when you had moments of deep appreciation for others, and when you experienced a deep sense of joy and connection with others. Imagine or recollect these memories of gratitude using all of your senses. Specifically try to bring in what you saw, emotionally felt, physically felt, heard, thought, smelled or tasted. Visualizing past experiences allows us to re-experience them. Flood your mind, body and consciousness with gratitude.

Day Three: Write in your journal today for 10 minutes without stopping. Start with the statement, "Today I am grateful for…"

Day Four: Repeat the journaling exercise from yesterday. Remember, in life whatever you focus on you attract. A gratitude journal is a powerful way of saturating your consciousness with thoughts of gratitude, which attracts more of what you are grateful for into your life.

Day Five: Tell at least one person you are grateful for them today. Be extremely specific for what and why you are grateful for and why you are blessed to have them in your life.

Day Six: Write a letter to someone who has had a positive impact on your life. Express a heart felt appreciation to this person. Be specific about what they did that had a positive impact on you. Be specific about the lasting impact their generosity and kindness had on your life.

Day Seven: Repeat the visualization exercise from day two. This time go back as far in your life as you can to recollect people, things, experiences, occasions and accomplishments you are grateful for. Allow yourself to fully re-experience multiple vivid memories of gratitude.

Dr. Mike Davison, Kay Guzder

27. Love makes the world go around

A loving person lives in a loving world. A hostile person lives in a hostile world: Everyone you meet is your mirror.

—Ken Keyes, Jr.

Teach only love for that is what you are.

—A Course in Miracles

In *A Course in Miracles* it is suggested that there are only two emotions: Love and Fear. Love cultivates connection with others and deepens one's experience of personal peace. Fear blocks us from the experience of personal peace. Fear cultivates selfishness which prevents individuals from being present for others in a loving way. On the level of metaphor, fear leads to an experience of being a starving person on a planet with only one remaining crumb of food. The consciousness of fear leads to greediness and a mentality of "What's in it for me?". This is why fear is such a destructive emotion. Fear leads to feelings of scarcity and lack, which in the extreme can contribute to ruthless acts of greed and disregard for others. Only love can truly and completely help us transcend fear. Only love can help us see others and the world from the perspective of abundance and unlimited supply. Only love can help us connect with our true essence—personal peace.

Cultivating love involves cultivating the virtues of acceptance, patience and kindness. Cultivating love involves seeing the innocence of human consciousness. Cultivating love involves transcending boastfulness and envy. Love is never purely self-serving. Love does not contribute to acts of anger. Love does not lead to judgment. What love always does is protect, preserve, build trust, contributes to a desire to resolve difference with others, and a desire to be of service.

Love is a powerful force, the most powerful force in the universe. However, like any other powerful force or resource, it does not serve the greater good if it is not shared. You can't horde love. You can't hang onto love. There is an unlimited supply. Ultimately you have to share love to keep it flowing in your life. Look for opportunities to share love; opportunities big and small. Smile at someone. Compliment someone. Engage in random acts of love and kindness. Let someone else take the prize parking spot. Hold the door for someone. Pay the toll for the "stranger" in back of you.

Those who have learned to transcend fear and live their life from a position of love, live in a more loving world. That may sound strange, but I believe it is true. If you come at people with love, you are more likely to receive it. If you expect kindness from others, you are more likely to receive it. You see, as humans, we are a bit like "bad scientists". We go around looking for, creating, and arranging for situations or experiences to confirm our perspective or theories about ourselves, other people, or life itself. As the comedian Flip Wilson used to say: "What you see is what you get".

Dr. Mike Davison, Kay Guzder

This week's practices will make use of contemplative writing exercises to help you cultivate feelings of love and personal peace. Each day read the quote and silently contemplate it. Then write out your reflections. Consider what the quote means to you. How can you apply it to your life? Keep in mind that knowledge or information alone means little. The magic is in application. Take action. Make love your way of being.

Daily Practices

Day One: "There is more hunger for love and appreciation in this world than for bread".

—Mother Teresa

Day Two: "All love that has not friendship for its base, is like a mansion built upon the sand".

—Ella Wheeler Wilcox

Day Three: "Love is always bestowed as a gift—
Freely, willingly, and without expectation....
We don't love to be loved; we love to love".

—Leo Buscaglia

Day Four: "Spread love everywhere you go:
First of all in your own home.
Give love to your children,
To a wife or husband,
To a next-door neighbor.

—Mother Teresa

Day Five: "Love is the great miracle cure. Loving ourselves works miracles in our lives."

—Louise Hay

Day Six: "The best and most beautiful things in the world cannot be seen or even Touched—they must be felt with the heart."

—Helen Keller

Day Seven: Based on your comtemplative writing exercises, what conclusions have you come to about love? How can you be more loving? What would being more loving mean in your life?

28. Compassion

"Compassion and love is the source of external and internal peace.

We should think of compassion as being the preserve of the sacred. It is one of our basic human qualities."

—The Dalai Lama

Recently I had the good fortune to be invited by my daughter to attend a lecture at Loyola University in Chicago. The guest speaker was peace activist and Vietnamese monk, Thich Nhat Hanh. I had been reading his books for some time and was excited to see this man of peace and experience his words of wisdom first hand. While standing in a long line waiting to enter the auditorium where the lecture was to be held, I noticed how peaceful and happy everyone seemed. There was no pushing, shoving or complaining going on even though people had been lined up for over an hour. I sensed something was different from the usual impatient mood that people normally displayed while waiting in line that long to attend a program. When we finally made our way into what I thought was an auditorium, I was stunned to find out we were being seated in the University gymnasium. It was the only place on campus that had the capacity to hold such a large audience and every seat was sold out.

The milling sounds of the crowd as they made their way to their seats almost drowned out what was taking place on stage. As we entered the gymnasium we saw about thirty young monks dressed in their traditional garb of wine and gold colored robes. They were sitting on the floor of an elevated stage that was open on all four sides. Their soft chanting reminded me of an orchestra tuning up before a symphony. Much to my surprise there were no formal introductions and the program began before I realized what had happened. Thich Nhat Hanh had simply walked onstage, sat down among the monks and began chanting with them. The chanting continued for about fifteen minutes and intermittently you would hear the soft chiming of a temple bell. The audience continued to file in chatting and getting settled. Eventually people realized that Thich Nhat Hanh was on stage. The gymnasium became noticeably quieter until all you could hear was the drone of the air conditioners, the soft chanting and the sound of the small temple bell in the peace activist's hand. I don't know how many people were in that gymnasium that evening but I would venture to guess that there were thousands. People were mesmerized by this man's peaceful demeanor and I was in awe of the happiness radiating from his face.

When the chanting finished and the temple bell became silent, Thich Nhat Hanh smiled, greeting everyone in the audience, and welcomed us as his brothers and sisters. His voice was soft and melodious, yet somehow it carried. He told us how happy he was to be with all of us. For the remainder of the program the audience was very quiet and intent on hearing every word. People were trying to muffle their coughs and sit very still in their seats. Thich Nhat Hanh spoke about the rewards of living a compassionate life, that compassion is not simply love but a sense of concern and responsibility for others. To paraphrase, he said we need to see each other's suffering as our own. Compassion is a sense of caring and thinking about the welfare of others. It is the attitude that brings inner peace. Joy is compassion turned inward when you feel compassion toward yourself as well as for others. It is the end of a power struggle and the end of competition.

He spoke about how important it is for every human being to recognize the opportunity to practice being an advocate for peaceful coexistence and the reality that we all are interconnected to our fellow human beings, of the importance of continuing the quest of finding personal peace and making it a way of life by extending it toward others until it becomes peace among nations; that no matter what the circumstances are, no matter what kind of adversity you are facing. if you practice compassion, it will give you inner strength and happiness and then you will feel your life is useful.

He said we must practice patience and not get angry with those who harm us. Instead we must have compassion for them. However, this does not mean that we should allow them to harm us and let them do whatever they like to us. He warned that some people focus so much on their own lives they destroy their capacity for compassion. When this occurs the small problems appear to be gigantic problems and only bring about more unhappiness, frustration, insecurity, and fear. All human beings have an innate desire to overcome suffering and to find happiness. Although you may sometimes feel desperation in dealing with life's problems, that is because we are human beings, and we have ways to work on that. That is the gift of being a human being.

In closing, this gentle monk reminded us that because we have this capacity we must extend it also to the creatures of this earth. Life is just as dear to a mute creature as it is to man. Just as one wants happiness and fears pain, just as one wants to live and not to die, so do other creatures. Although we do not believe that trees or flowers have minds, we must also treat them with respect. We must share a sense of universal responsibility for mankind, all of earth's creatures and our environment. He reminded us that the overwhelming majority of people are engaged in acts of loving, caring and sharing. He encouraged us to try to be a nice person and reach out to one another, see another's suffering as our own.

As we were leaving the lecture on our way to the parking lot my daughter and I began sharing our feelings about the experience we had just witnessed. We felt as if we had been awash in a river of peace, it was flowing through us and we wanted to stay in the flow. There was a similar air of tranquility between all of the people we encountered along the way as we made our way to our car. We felt connected to everyone in the audience and to the peaceful monks on stage and to our teacher, Thich Nhat Hanh. We wanted to keep that peaceful feeling and experience with us and practice the virtue of compassion in our lives to help us continue to hold on to the feelings of peace and happiness that we had experienced in the gymnasium that night.

That evening, as I listened to Thich Nhat Hanh talk about the importance of practicing the virtue of compassion as the key to personal peace and peaceful coexistence I was reminded of a story that I read about him a long time ago. That memory resonated with me that night and helped me to comprehend the true meaning of compassion as an action and not just as rhetoric. I would like to share this story with you as a way of closing this chapter so that you can have a deeper understanding of the enormous healing power inherent in the practice of compassion.

During the Viet Nam War, Thich Nhat Hanh was a teacher and the spiritual leader of a group of young novice monks at a monastery in Viet Nam. He lived under very difficult circumstances trying to maintain and teach his beliefs related to peaceful and compassionate coexistence. He was under suspicion and surveillance by both the Viet Cong and the American military because he refused to take sides in the conflict and declare allegiance to either side. Eventually his duties required him to travel away from his home monastery to teach other student monks at outlying locations. While he was away a terrible tragedy took place. When he returned he found all his novice monks slaughtered and left lying in the courtyard. He was the only one left. He did not know who was responsible for this terrible act. He later wrote about this experience saying "I had to bury my young monks and find forgiveness in my heart for those who did this." This was the only way out of the tragedy for him. He was saved by his belief that compassion was more than a belief; it was a belief that led to action. After an assassination attempt on his life, Thich Nhat Hahn left Viet Nam and found refuge in France. He maintains his residence there in the countryside at a place called, "Plum Village." The peace advocates, nuns, and monks grow plums and make jam to sell. The money generated from their work and from Thich Nhat Hanh's lectures is used to support the victims of war, the widows and orphans in Viet Nam including those children of mixed Vietnamese and American ethnicity who are rejected as outcasts and are considered neither Vietnamese nor American.

As you can see, the story did not end with the burial of those novice monks in the courtyard. The incident was transformed from one of tragedy to one of hope. Thich Nhat Hanh was nominated for the Nobel Peace Prize by Dr. Martin Luther King Jr. and was invited to participate as a delegate to the Paris Peace Talks. His work continues as he writes books, travels and lectures all over the world as an advocate for peace. Thich Nhat Hanh suffered immeasurably from the loss of his loved ones and his homeland yet he continues to live and teach the deeper meaning and importance of living a life of love and compassion for all of humanity and all the creatures of this earth.

It is my hope that this story will help open your eyes, your heart, and your mind, as it did mine, to the healing powers of compassion practiced in your daily life. The 15-minute daily practices that follow are designed to allow you to experience the true deeper meaning of compassion as you find your personal peace living your life as an advocate for others to learn the lessons of Thich Nhat Hanh.

Daily Practices

Day One: Write a few paragraphs in your journal about your understanding of the concept of compassion.

Day Two: Spend a few minutes reflecting on the concept of practicing compassion as a tool for healing and finding personal peace. Write a few paragraphs in your journal about how you might apply this to your own personal circumstances.

Day Three: Consider the story of the slaughter in the courtyard and the importance of finding forgiveness as the way to move beyond difficult situations. Write a few paragraphs about compassion being more than a belief; it is a belief that leads to action.

Day Four: Thich Nhat Hanh stresses the importance of recognizing we are interconnected to our fellow human beings and we must recognize the opportunity to practice being an advocate for peaceful coexistence. Write a few paragraphs about how you will continue your quest to find personal peace and make it a way of life by extending it toward others.

Day Five: An important lesson is being taught in Thich Nhat Hanh's warning to us that some people focus so much on their own lives they destroy their capacity for compassion. He cautions that when this occurs small problems appear to be gigantic and only bring about more unhappiness, frustration, insecurities and fears. Spend a few minutes reflecting and journaling about specific times in the past when you have been so focused on the problems of life that you lost sight of the logical resolutions that were available to you. Did your approach continue to complicate your life further?

Day Six: Spend a few minutes writing about how to begin making changes in your life by practicing the expanded concept of compassion. Be specific about how you will continue your quest to bring personal peace into your life and how you will extend yourself to be an advocate for peaceful coexistence.

Day Seven: Spend some time meditating on the practice of compassion as it applies to finding inner peace and happiness. Reflect on the idea that it takes courage and strength of character to practice forgiveness and compassion. Ask yourself if there are any circumstances in your life that need to be addressed? Do you see a way to use the concept of forgiveness and compassion in resolving conflict situations? Write a plan in your journal about how you will begin to incorporate these concepts into your life so that you can move beyond difficult situations instead of remaining stuck in negative emotions.

29. Living a life of contribution

"Be constantly aware of the need to serve God and serve others in any and all of your actions. That is the way of the miracle worker."

—Dr. Wayne Dyer

I would like to share with you some words of wisdom written by three different authors who I consider to be miracle workers. They convey their message simply and beautifully, giving us something to think about, something to keep for ourselves and something to give to others.

First I have chosen excerpts from a poem entitled, "About Things That Matter" written by the late Mattie J. T. Stepanek. Mattie became a New York Times bestselling author and poet at the age of eleven. This poem is found in his book *Celebrate Through Heartsongs*. He was the 2002 National Goodwill Ambassador for the Muscular Dystrophy Association.

"It matters that the world knows we must celebrate the gift of life, everyday in some way.

It matters that the world knows all children are truly blessed with the innocent gifts of gentleness, trust and compassion, which should guide the wisdom of grown-ups.

It matters that the world knows we must choose our words and wants carefully or we could forever hurt others with these most dangerous weapons.

It matters that the world knows a person by my name and being existed with a strong spirit and an eternal mindset to become a peacemaker for all by sharing the things that really matter."

Next is the "G.U.I.D.E. To Soulful Giving" by Linda R. Harper from her book *Give To Your Heart's Content*.

"Give wholly to yourself the seeds of giving, start with paying attention to your needs."

"Unconditionally choose to give. Give without strings attached. Be open to the surprises of giving freely."

"Integrate your unique gifts. Recognize and honor your abilities and limitations."

"Delight in the act of giving. Enjoy the process, let go of the outcome."

"Experience the expanding capacity to give. Soulful giving keeps on growing!"

Finally, from Gregg Braden, New York Times best selling author and leading authority on the ancient applications of spirituality and technology, as the closing statement of his conference entitled "Living In The Mind Of God"

"Use the gift of your life wisely."

As you contemplate the words of wisdom from these three writers, consider the concept of living a life of contribution. A lot of people make a contribution by writing a check to a charitable organization. Some open wide their wallets during holidays and make a difference in the lives of those less fortunate. Some people give up the idea of making a contribution entirely because they don't feel that small contributions make a difference or they worry that the money will be misused. While advocating making charitable monetary donations, there are other benefits to be derived from giving in different ways that don't require you to rearrange your budget. Think about the possibility that exists to make a significant contribution on a daily basis to your fellow human beings. All that is required is to make a simple shift in the way we think and act in our daily lives, wherever we are and with whomever you encounter along the way.

Begin by acknowledging the contributions you are already making in your daily life and ask yourself how you can expand and extend those gifts with a spirit of increasing generosity. For example, consider ways that you contribute to the well-being of your family. Extend that to include the contributions you make in the workplace. For instance, if you are a mechanic consider how much you contribute to your employer by being a person that can be counted on to show up and do a good job each day. Your work makes it possible for your employer to contribute in their field of expertise. The operation runs smoothly when the employer and employee support each other and care about the quality of the service that is being delivered to the consumer. Add to this your capacity to work responsibly, cooperate and be friendly and you have expanded your contribution threefold. As you experience the good feelings of making a worthwhile contribution you will find it easier to incorporate this way of thinking and behaving into your daily interactions in other areas of your life. As you go about your daily life, everyone you encounter benefits from your contribution.

Consider the contributions of the homemaker. Think about how people in this role create a safe secure place in which others are nurtured and guided. Homemakers provide the base from which family members go to school or the workplace. The breadwinners and students can emulate the lessons of the homemaker by developing their own capacity to make new contributions to society. Each person expands the capacity of the group to enhance the lives of one another. Imagine you could incorporate the hobbies you are passionate about into a contribution. This could further develop your capacity for giving. Suppose you love to grow strawberries and make jam. You could enjoy growing the berries, making the jam and you could enhance your joy by donating some jars to the senior citizens center in your hometown. You get a sense of satisfaction from doing something you love and you get a sense of well being from sharing with others. Everyone benefits especially those who give of themselves.

World renowned psychiatrist, Dr. Alfred Adler, gave this advice to his depressed patients:

> "If everyday for the next two weeks you do something nice for someone else with no thought of secondary gain or personal reward, you will be cured of your depression and you won't have to come see me any more!"

Think about incorporating these ideas into your daily encounters as you go about your day. Give yourself credit for the contributions you make to your family, your work, and to society. Pat yourself on the back and then ask yourself what else you would like to do to experience the sense of satisfaction that comes from making a difference in the lives of others. Become aware that life is better because you make a contribution to the well-being of others and to yourself. Gregg Braden's quote carries a strong message that bears repeating:

> "Use the Gift of Your Life Wisely."

Daily Practices

Day One: Spend some time journaling how you contribute to the well being of your family. Write about how your job contributes to your employer.

Day Two: Spend some time reflecting and journaling on the concept of celebrating your gift of life.

Day Three: Spend some time reflecting on your unique talents. Use this awareness to help yourself write in your journal. Try to gain a clearer understanding of how to create ways to contribute. Ask yourself if there is a way to cooperate with others who have talents different from yours? Are there ways to combine talents to make a two-fold contribution?

Day Four: Spend some time journaling about a specific plan of action and a time frame for implementing your new ideas. Write about ideas that excite you. What are you passionate about? What unique talents do you have that you want to include in the plan.

Day Five: Use your imagination today. What do you wish someone would have done for you when you were a kid? Write about it. Can you build on this idea and think of ways to make a contribution that would really get you excited?

Day Six: Write a few paragraphs about how people sometimes diminish and discount the usefulness of their talents. Ask yourself if you have this tendency? Do you have handy excuses for why you can't initiate a plan for making small changes in your routine that would include extending yourself to others? If you find yourself hanging back and dragging your feet about this assignment remind yourself that small contributions do count and if you begin living a life of contribution, a life of giving without strings attached, you will find great satisfaction in knowing that you made a difference in the lives of others because you walked the face of this earth.

Day Seven: Spend some time journaling about how you will begin to implement steps toward creating a life of contribution. Finish today's journaling by writing a paragraph starting with the sentence, *"Some Ways That I Can Use the Gift of My Life Wisely Are...."*.

30. Keeping peace in our hearts

"Our capacity to make peace with another person and with the world depends very much on our capacity to make peace with ourselves."

—Thich Nhat Hanh

"Lord make me an instrument of your peace,
Where there is hatred, let me sow love..."

—St. Francis of Assisi

While struggling with three very troubling incidents a few years back I found myself obsessing over the offending situations without coming to any useful resolution. I felt stressed to the max, angry, frustrated, resentful, and one particular situation had me feeling hopeless and despondent. I tried my best to find my balance and some objectivity around these issues but for some reason this time, I felt overwhelmed and deeply challenged as I was unable to get to a place of resolution and peace. The same techniques I had used in the past were somehow eluding me.

Dr. Mike Davison, Kay Guzder

The most troubling of these issues had to do with witnessing a particularly angry and hurtful encounter between two family members that I dearly love. It was a verbal exchange that nearly came to blows. I was getting ready to leave for a conference and I wondered if I would be able to concentrate and get anything out of it. As I pulled out of my driveway I remember feeling sad and discouraged. Normally, I'm pretty upbeat and can pull something good out of most negative situations. This time I could see nothing positive. As I drove toward Atlanta to pick up my sister who was accompanying me to the seminar, I wondered if my despondent mood would lessen. Would I be putting a damper on our long anticipated plans to attend this seminar together? By the time I got to Georgia I knew I had to tell my sister about what was deeply troubling me. I knew I could count on her gentle wisdom to help me find clarity and direction. I filled her in on the details of problems I was facing and after listening to my concerns she said, "Don't worry, the conference we are about to attend will help you find the answers. The conference is called "Living in The Mind of God" and the answers are there." My sister had attended this conference once before and was so impressed with the facilitator that she wanted me to have the same first-hand experience as she had.

The seminar was incredible. The featured speaker, Gregg Braden, is a former Senior Computer Systems Designer for Martin Marietta Aerospace, Computer geologist for Phillips Petroleum, and the Technical Operations Manager for Cisco Systems. Braden is considered a pioneer in bridging the wisdom of our past with the science, healing and peace of our future. Dr. Deepak Chopra, in a testimonial to Braden's work writes, "He is a rare blend of scientist, visionary and scholar, with the ability to speak to our minds, while touching the wisdom of our hearts." Gregg Braden's work at Martin Marietta put him in contact with many of the space program astronauts, including those who had traveled to the moon. He had the opportunity to talk with them upon completion of their missions. Their mutual interests in science and spirituality prompted him to ask specific questions about their experience while in outer space and after returning to earth. They all expressed similar feelings about their experience of the universe from outer space and how it deepened their spiritual belief system. They felt the connection to the universe and its creator as never before and it had changed their lives.

In the seminar Braden spoke about the realization that as science comes closer to understanding the universe and its creation, we come closer to an understanding of the Mind of God. He talked about an ancient religious sect, the Essenes, who had an understanding about the relationship between man and God that modern science is only recently "discovering" within the field of quantum physics. He presented this material explaining that much of this knowledge has been described in the writings of ancient religions including the Bible, the Dead Sea Scrolls, and in other sacred books and philosophies throughout the world. Braden believes that we are all united through the matrix of the creator and that as we grow closer to understanding creation we grow closer to the God of our understanding.

Braden travels throughout the world, studying and sharing these concepts in his seminars. Basic to his teaching is the idea that each of us has a profound affect on our environment. We impact the energy field that surrounds us either in a negative or positive way by the thoughts and emotions that we have. He uses solid scientific research to show how our thoughts have long range and lasting effects on our fellow human beings. Much to my surprise and delight, Braden presented material that blended and reiterated what I had learned and practiced from books written by Thich Nhat Hanh. He quoted him many times and supported his work promoting world peace. He told the audience that Thich Nhat Hanh was nominated by Dr. Martin Luther King, Jr. for the Nobel Peace Prize and was invited to be a key speaker at the Paris Peace Talks and has dedicated his life to promoting world peace. The similarity between Thich Nhat Hanh and Martin Luther King, Jr. is unmistakable. Both men dedicated their lives to working to promote world peace and more importantly they had each found personal peace in the midst of the adversarial and violent times they lived in. In the worst of circumstances, each of them generated consistent messages of hope and love to all they encountered. Their positive thoughts related to creating peaceful social and personal change have had profound effects on millions of people throughout the world.

Over the course of the weekend, Braden presented research results from projects conducted by US Army scientists, Carl Sagen, and other respected scientists and researchers. The hypothesis of these researchers is that individuals impact their environment either in a positive or negative way by the thoughts and emotions they have from moment to moment. These thoughts and emotions send out vibrations into the electrical field that surrounds each of us. The vibration waves are not unlike radio waves and microwaves, and the result is that our thoughts and emotions impact the world around us for distances far beyond our immediate environment and far beyond what we ever imagined. In fact, research indicates that even at a molecular level an individual's positive or negative emotions are having an impact on fostering violence or peace in our own bodies. As an example, Braden presented results from a research project in which scientists wanted to know what happens to statistics on violent crime when people are participating collectively using group prayer to promote peace. They wanted to see if group prayer over a 60-day time period would have a measurable impact statistically on violent crime in several major cities around the world. The researchers contacted existing prayer groups and, over that time period, monitored major violent crime statistics for those cities. They found that during the 60-day time period the incidence of violent crime was reduced significantly and on the 61st day after the group prayers ceased, rates of violent crime returned to their original levels.

When the attacks on the World Trade Center occurred on September 11, 2001, the scientists took the opportunity to go back several days before the 11th and examine the statistics. They found that in the week prior to the attack they were near baseline average level for New York City. As each day progressed toward the 11th, the measures began to rise. On September 9th and 10th they spiked to the top of the charts, and fell off drastically on the 11th. Clearly this experiment supports the hypothesis of the existence of strong emotions impacting over time and space, both negative and positive. Considering the serious implications of this research are we not morally obliged to contemplate our individual contributions as people either dedicated to promoting peace in our surroundings and in our universe or projecting violence?

Gregg Braden continues to travel and lecture worldwide to present evidence linking science and spirituality as a potent tool in the search for world peace. He inspires his audiences to look at themselves as instruments of peace, to become aware at how negative emotions impact on us individually and then are projected outward to our fellow beings and our universe.

While driving home my sister and I discussed how the conference had affected us. I was feeling a tremendous sense of relief in the realization that my responsibility is to maintain peace and positive thoughts and emotions in my being. I realized that in doing so, I will positively impact my family, friends and the world around me. Upon returning home I met individually with my family members and shared some of the new ideas I had learned at the conference. I told them that I had found a way to keep peace in my heart and that this concept would be my roadmap in all of my actions, decisions and interactions from now on. I decided to incorporate peaceful prayer, hope and love into my daily life. I created a sacred space in my home to remind me of my practice. It became clear to me that in following my pathway to peaceful daily living I had found the tools that would enable me to make the right decisions to resolve complex emotional issues regardless of whether they were internal or external in my life. I am happy to report that my loved ones have peacefully reconciled their differences and have joined me in this collective peaceful approach. They found a way to lay down their arms and keep peace in their hearts, minds and relationships. You can do this too.

MAY THE FORCE BE WITH YOU!

Daily Practices

Day One: Spend some time today reflecting on how negative emotions impact you in your daily life.

Day Two: Spend some time journaling about how you express your negative emotions and how it makes you feel. Note how your body feels after encountering negative emotions? Where do you harbor negative emotions in your body? Do you feel them in the pit of your stomach? Do you get a tightening in your chest? Do you get a headache? Are your fists clenched? Is your jaw tight? Do you feel the tension in the muscles of your entire body as if engaged in a battle? Write about how stress and tension impacts on all the systems of the body. Include a few of your own thoughts about the material presented by Gregg Braden about how far negative emotions can travel.

Day Three: Think about a specific problem you have been struggling with. Write a few paragraphs about how you might apply the idea of keeping peace in your heart to find a peaceful solution to your conflict.

Days Four and Five: Refer back to yesterday journaling exercise and read what you wrote about keeping peace in your heart as a way to find a peaceful solution to your conflict situation. Pay attention to how your positive thoughts lead you to positive feelings and emotions. Notice how you feel physically, as you begin to let positive emotions lead you toward a path of peaceful resolution. Write in your journal about any new thoughts or insights you discover.

Day Six: Write a few paragraphs in your journal about how you can apply some of the concepts you have read about in this chapter to help you find peaceful resolutions to your particular conflicts. Write about some negative encounters you have experienced in your dealings with others, for example family members, friends or coworkers. Write a new plan of action to help yourself keep peace in your heart as you make your move toward addressing the conflicts. Keep in mind that in times of stress it is all the more important to keep a cool head through keeping peace in your heart.

Day Seven: Today take a spiritual walk in peaceful silence and meditate about what you have learned from your daily practices this week. Let these discoveries permeate your thoughts and then go home and make yourself a cup of "peaceful tea" to celebrate your journey of discovery. If tea is not "your cup of tea", then brew a pot of coffee and call it your "sacred grounds". While savoring your special treat make the choice to keep peace in your heart as a way of life.

31. Emptiness

"Through the practice of meditation upon emptiness, one generates a store of wisdom, and through the other practices, such as benefiting others and meditating on compassion, one generates a great store of creative energy."

—The Dalai Lama

In our culture thoughts and feelings relating to the concept of emptiness conjure up visions of isolation, loneliness, or loss of direction. It is perceived as a negative state, something to be avoided. In consulting the dictionary for the complete definition of the concept of emptiness, you find an explanation which presents the positive component of emptiness, "to remove from what holds and encloses". We can all relate to how good it feels to clean out a cluttered closet or a junk drawer, to experience that feeling of having a new start, a feeling of freedom. The idea of getting rid of clutter relates to the positive concept of emptiness. It creates a clear space that can be used for a more useful purpose. Meditating allows you to empty your mind of mental clutter and make room for positive nurturing thoughts and actions thus creating the potential for true happiness and peace.

Reflect for a moment on the day you were born. Throughout

infancy and early childhood your life can be compared to a pristine pond. Initially you look into your pond and see your reflection clearly, but somehow over time, the pond becomes polluted. Imagine that with each passing day a little bit of toxic waste is dumped into our pond, and we notice that the pond is becoming cloudy and less clear. Sometimes we do the dumping and sometimes someone or something else pollutes our pond. It doesn't matter how the pond gets polluted, what matters is that we take steps to clean it up so we can see our true reflections clearly. We may decide that in order to find our true selves, our clear and reflected image, we must begin by draining our pond so that we can refill it with positive, pure, pristine thoughts, ideas and plans which allow us to experience peaceful, fulfilling, meaningful lives.

The purpose of pursuing emptiness is to empty ourselves of our false toxic self. Too many of us are "so full of ourselves" that there is no room for anything else. We get so self-focused, self-centered and self-absorbed that we lose sight of our true nature and how to live a life of lasting peace and harmony.

A dear friend of mine, Maryann Narveson, a talented potter, artist, author and teacher, shared this story with me. Once upon a time, a young novice Buddhist monk approached his teacher lamenting the fact that he had studied for many months and had studied longer and harder than others to attain the knowledge that would let him graduate to a higher level of understanding. He felt somehow dissatisfied that he was not able to grasp the feeling of having mastered the lessons. His teacher invited him to his home for tea so they could ponder the student's dilemma together. Upon entering the teacher's home, the student was invited to take tea with the master. The table was set with the teapot and cups. The student was instructed to begin pouring the tea into a cup.

As he poured, the cup began to fill and the teacher instructed him to keep pouring. Soon the teacup was filled to the brim, but the teacher told him to keep pouring. When the tea spilled onto the table and the floor the student became upset and shouted, "What are you doing? Why do you ask me to keep pouring when the cup is full and the tea is running onto the table and floor?" The teacher replied "Now you can see the lesson. You are like the tea in the teacup. You are overflowing but you do not empty yourself before you try to put in more!"

The lesson here is to experience the positive nature of emptiness, to empty out the clutter so you can begin to contemplate and recognize how you want to replenish yourself and get back to your pristine pond. The answers we are looking for are not far away. They are not hidden. They are just out of our awareness. We have become accustomed to multitasking to keep ourselves distracted. We are so busy that we lose our potential for reflecting on our lives, of seeing our true reflection.

Visit your pond frequently to see if it is polluted or pristine. Is it reflecting clearly or in a distorted fashion? Is it filled with misperceptions and misgivings, or is it allowing you to take a look at new ideas that will nourish you on you path to peace? Aspire to experience the wellspring of the empty mind, that emptiness which removes you from what holds and encloses you.

Daily Practices

Day One: Reflect on the concept of emptiness and empty mind. Write in your journal about the positive ways that emptiness prepares you to create new opportunities to experience peace in your life.

Day Two: Journal about your understanding of the concept of emptiness. How does it differ from your definition of emptiness before you read the above essay?

Day Three: Reflect and journal about the ways you keep clutter in your life, both mentally and physically. Seek to understand how clutter blocks your ability to bring positive nourishing thoughts and actions into your daily life.

Day Four: Imagine looking into your personal pond. Write a description in your journal of how your pond appears to you. Is it clear or polluted? What does it reflect? Do you see your reflection as positive or negative? Expand on this as you write. Let your thoughts flow freely. See what you can learn about yourself from your writing. Remember it is your writing and you can decide if you want to share it with someone or not.

Day Five and Six: Reflect on the story of the tea lesson. Journal about how you fill your mind and life. Pay particular attention to how you spend your time. Do you keep yourself busy with thoughts about yourself? Do you distract yourself by making comparisons with others? Do your thoughts lead to actions that are harmful or helpful to you and your fellow human beings? Ask if you need to empty yourself of overflow? What would help you clear your mind so you could make the move to the next level of growth? Write a few paragraphs about what thoughts came up for you as you completed this practice.

Day Seven: Today spend some time identifying one specific problem that you have wanted to solve for some time. Clean out some clutter, either from your environment or from your mind and begin to journal about the new ideas and solutions being generated regarding solving this specific problem.

Think about what you have done previously as you tried to address this issue and write a new plan of action. Write about this experience and what you have learned from this practice.

Dr. Mike Davison, Kay Guzder

✳

Section V. Connecting with Your Big Picture

32. Creating a purpose statement

"Your vision will become clear only when you look into your heart. Who looks outside, dreams. Who looks inside, awakens."

—Carl Jung

I strongly believe everyone has a purpose or reason they were placed on this planet. I personally have not reconciled the issue of whether one's life purpose is divinely inspired or if it is of our own choosing. However, I am certain that through the process of self-reflection, contemplation, prayer and consultation with others we can discern how to live our lives in the most purposeful and meaningful way.

There is tremendous power in creating a written document that can be best thought of as a purpose statement. It is best to look at your purpose statement as a fluid and evolving document. Your life purpose is not fixed or static. We certainly are not fixed or static beings. A purpose statement simply documents your purpose in life and how you will play out your life's purpose. Your purpose statement answers such questions as: Who am I? What are my values? How am I going to use my time in the service of my life's purpose?

In the process of writing a purpose statement I have some ideas that have worked for me. One is to keep it brief. By this I mean a paragraph or two. I think it should be peppered with language that is inspiring to you. I also believe that it should include how living your most purposeful life will contribute to the lives of others. Living your life's purpose involves connecting with something beyond you; something bigger than you.

Once you complete your purpose statement, you should refer to the statement on a regular basis, perhaps even daily. I also think you should consider revisions at least once a year. A purpose statement ultimately gives you a springboard to evaluate yourself to determine if you are on track in life. Your purpose statement allows you to create your short- and long-term goals. A purpose statement also helps you schedule your time each day in a way that is congruent with your highest personal priorities. This sort of alignment will allow you to feel a profound level of clarity, certainty, fulfillment, and inspiration. This will allow personal peace to more effortlessly unfold in your life.

Daily Practices

Day One: Are you clear about the kind of person you want to be?

In your journal, write out your responses to the statements below to get clearer about their life's purpose.

My life's purpose is...

My empowering self-definition is...

I want my life to be an answer to what question?

My personal purpose statement is...

The sort of influence on others I'd like to be is…

Day Two: Today complete the following sentence stems:

My life is about…

What I stand for is…

Also identify what you are willing to do on the level of your behavior to have your life be consistent with your responses.

Day Three: Imagine that it is your 90th birthday and you are asked by the President of the United States to address the nation on primetime television to speak about what is most important to you. What would you talk about?

Day Four: While this one may sound a bit morbid to some, go with it anyway. Write your own eulogy. Write it in the 3rd person as if someone else is writing it about you. Specifically identify the impact you had, the values you stood for and the legacy that you will leave behind. Cover all domains of life; your family life, your career, your community life, your spirituality, and any other important areas of influence.

Day Five: Reflect on the eulogy you wrote yesterday. Think about how you can leverage the eulogy to hold yourself to a higher standard in your own life.

Day Six: Review your journal from this week. In reflecting upon all of what you wrote and all of what you connected with, write a one-paragraph purpose statement for your life. Don't worry about getting it perfect, you can always update, modify, or expand upon what you wrote at a later date.

Day Seven: Share your purpose statement with someone. Also put it somewhere, such as your daily planner, so you can review it daily.

33. The five tasks of life

"You must give something to your fellow man—even if it is a little thing, do something for others—something for which you get no pay but the privilege of doing it."

—Dr. Albert Schweitzer

When I was a graduate student at The Adler School of Professional Psychology, one of my favorite professors, Dr. John Neubauer, was lecturing on the Adlerian theory that people who want to live happy, healthy, purposeful and productive lives, must master the five tasks of life. These five areas are *work, friendship, intimacy, spirituality and universal connectedness*. He clarified by explaining that the task of work means being engaged in some form of career or employment that provides for our financial welfare. In turn, your job contributes to your fellow man and makes a meaningful contribution to society.

The task of friendship, creating and maintaining friendships in your life, must be mastered so you can remain connected to your fellow beings in mutually cooperative relationships to overcome loneliness and isolation.

The task of creating intimacy requires you to get involved and stay emotionally connected to a significant other to give

Dr. Mike Davison, Kay Guzder

and receive love and to procreate. People who choose to live single lives, those who choose to remain celibate as part of a religious order, and individuals in long term same sex relationships, are called upon to master this task as well.

The task of spirituality refers to your connection to other human beings and to a higher creative power. For most of us the guide for exploring and expanding our individual beliefs related to matters of spirituality comes from the religious traditions taught to us in our family of origin. As mature adults, most people develop a concept of the God of their understanding and their relationship to their God. Some choose a more secular belief system that connects them spiritually to the universe by their place in nature and its delicate balance and infinite wisdom.

The final task of life, universal connectedness, as described by my professor, is to reach an understanding that we are part of a vast universe and interconnected to all other life forms that exist in this system. He explained that we're intrinsically connected to everything and everybody, from the smallest molecule here on earth to the galaxies far beyond our telescopes and comprehension. To clarify this concept he gave a wonderful example. He noticed one student wearing a strand of pearls and asked where she got them. She replied that her mother had given them to her. He then asked where her mother got them. She replied they had been given to her mother by her grandmother. He asked how her grandmother got the pearls and the student replied "From my grandfather." He asked, "How did your grandfather get the pearls?" She answered, "At a jewelry store." He asked "Where did the jeweler get the pearls?" "From a buyer, I suppose." she continued. He pressed further, "Where did the buyer get them?", "I guess from a supplier overseas somewhere." He asked, "How about the supplier, where did he get them?" "From a pearl diver," "Where did the pearl diver get the pearls?" And now the enlightened student smiled and replied, "From an oyster in the bottom of the ocean". Dr Neubauer relished the moment and replied, "Now you see how you are connected to the oysters in the bottom of the ocean that gave you those pearls on through every one in the chain of events. You are connected to your mother, her mother, your grandfather, the jeweler, the buyer, the supplier, the diver and the oysters." When you understand this and apply it universally it becomes clear that we are all a part of, and interconnected to, everything in the universe. Understanding this concept makes it more difficult to remain disconnected and separate. Hostility or apathy toward other beings ultimately affects us. When we understand the concept of universal connectedness, we begin to understand we cannot ignore hostility and violence against others as a normal everyday occurrence that has no impact on us.

In order to live a peaceful existence we need to understand that it is necessary to make a contribution; stay connected to others through maintaining friendships and intimate relations, develop and foster our spiritual life, and always be mindful of our connection to the universe as a whole.

What an incredible and valuable lesson given to all thirty graduate students that day in an introductory class on Adlerian theory. You can take these lessons and apply them on your journey to bring peace into your life and extend that peace to the universe you are part of. You can recognize the many connections you have to your fellow beings and evaluate how you are contributing to benefit others. Do you see your work as a task that you resent or as an opportunity to make a useful contribution yourself and to the wellbeing of others? Are you self absorbed or do can you reach out to others in helpful ways? When you are aware of your inter-connectedness to others throughout the world, you are less likely to inflict emotional and physical pain on others. You can become aware of how you relate to your universe by taking stock of how you interact with others and your natural environment. Are you wasteful and destructive in your inter-actions with the gifts of nature? We are all a small part of the same planet. You can find peace in preserving and protecting the natural beauty of the world. As you incorporate the above concepts into your daily life you will move naturally along the path that leads you to a place of peace in your life.

Daily Practices

Day One: Spend some time thinking about your work and how it reflects your talents and contributes to your well being and that of the community you live in. Write a few paragraphs about your attitude toward your work life and the areas in which you want to grow and develop.

Day Two: Spend some time reflecting and journaling about the friendships you have and how you can nurture these rela-tionships. Ask yourself if you are cooperative or competitive in your relationships? How much time do you devote to nur-turing your relationships?

Day Three: Spend some time evaluating the intimate rela-tionships you have in your life and whether you are open and trusting within your closest relationships. Think about ways in which your most intimate relationships allow you to develop and grow toward living a life of peace.

Day Four: Spend some time reflecting and journaling about the God of your understanding and how you are spiritually connected to something larger than yourself. Think about how this spiritual connection fosters a sense of peace in your daily life.

Day Five: Spend some time contemplating how you are connected to the earth that sustains you; and to the sun, air and water that gives you life. Do you take these gifts for granted or do you think of them as gifts that are to be treasured and protected? Think about how you will pass these gifts on to future generations. Will they be worn and tattered or will they be more beautiful than they were when you first received them?

Day Six: Spend some time journaling about how you are doing in all five life task areas. Determine which areas are in need of attention so that you can achieve balance and be at peace in your life.

Day Seven: Reflect and give thanks for the gifts in your life that allow you to contemplate, write and appreciate your existence as part of a universal plan. Bask in the glow of your social connections and give thanks that you belong to a family, a community, a country and the universe. Celebrate how you have learned to think and develop your thoughts to have a deeper connection to yourself and your universe.

May peace be with you.

Dr. Mike Davison, Kay Guzder

34. Choosing to live a purposeful and meaningful life

"Authentic empowerment is knowing that you are on purpose doing God's work peacefully and harmoniously."

—Dr. Wayne Dyer

What makes your life worth living? What is your purpose on earth? What gives meaning to your life? What are you passionate about? I am not referring to the passion associated with romance and sexuality but rather the kind of passion Wilbur Wright, the pioneer in aviation spoke of when he said, "We could hardly wait to get up in the morning." And, given your "druthers" you'd "druther" be doing this than anything else. If you are lucky enough to be this passionate about your work you might be thinking "I would do this everyday even if I didn't get paid to do it." If you can put that kind of passion into something that connects you to your fellow human beings and makes a useful contribution to society, you would be living a purposeful meaningful life.

I was listening to poet and writer, Dr. Maya Angelou, on

National Public Radio and the commentator asked her what her formula was for living a fulfilled and happy life. She imparted these words of wisdom, "Wake up in the morning and celebrate life. Celebrate that you're alive and leave the poison behind. If you're not complaining, then you're celebrating. Celebrate and percolate. Live your life with passion and purpose. Never compete with anyone but yourself."

While Dr. Angelou's thoughts are a sure formula for successful living, you might be asking yourself, "How does this apply to my life? How do I create more purpose, meaning and passion in my daily life? How do I evaluate what changes I want to make? What choices do I have to make to create a life worth celebrating?

Begin by taking some time to reflect on how you use the talents you have been given. Do you use your talents to benefit others? Is your attitude one of apathy that reflects an attitude that you don't matter? Do you recognize the importance of small gestures that can mean a great deal in the grand scheme of things? For example, mothers, fathers and grandparents caring for their children and teaching them the morals and values that make a vital contribution to the next generation. Or actions such as extending yourself by coaching a little league team or cleaning up a park or neighborhood, volunteering at an animal shelter, or conserving energy and water. This is the embodiment of the slogan, "Think Globally, Act Locally!" You can contemplate and evaluate yourself to determine how you want to make a difference in the world. In doing so you must be willing to recognize your unique gifts and talents and then determine how you want to use them to benefit yourself and others. Ask yourself if you are acting one dimensionally and using your talents only to gain wealth or personal power, or if you could direct some of your energy toward helping others? Choosing to expand

and extend your gifts and talents toward helping your fellow beings gives you the roadmap and direction you need to find a life filled with purpose and meaning. This soul searching results in life choices that make sense. It allows your passion to flow into the world in a way that makes a difference to others and enables you to be true to yourself and your values.

By creating a life with purpose and meaning you experience feelings of being worthwhile and significant. You live your life joined with others and leave a legacy when you are gone. Your legacy could be, "The world is a better place because I walked the face of the earth. I made my contributions willingly, without resentment. Having lived my life in this way, I left the earth having no regrets, for my life was well spent, happy and complete."

Daily Practices

Day One: Spend some time reflecting on how your life relates to your values and the things you care most about. Do you feel excited at the start of the day and fulfilled at the end, or is each day lived like an assembly line of meaningless tasks producing apathy and dread as you face the future?

Day Two: Spend some time journaling about what is important to you, what do you value in the world and what is your purpose is in it.

Day Three: Today write a mission statement for your life. Include a statement about your purpose in life and the contribution you can make to others.

Day Four: Spend some time reflecting about the things in your life that you are most passionate about. Think about your childhood and what you really enjoyed doing. Include your adult and childhood passions when you write these thoughts in your journal

Day Five: Spend some time making a list of your strengths and talents. This exercise will help you develop a stronger sense of yourself and the contributions you can make to improve the world you live in. It is the opposite of boasting or bragging, it is about what you can contribute.

Day Six: Reflect and journal on what is standing in the way of putting your good, creative ideas into action. Dispute your negative perceptions and think about taking steps to move in a positive direction. Incorporate the idea that success is achieved by making small changes in the right direction over time.

Day Seven: Today, take whatever time you need to write a list of ways you can choose to create a more purposeful and meaningful life Ask yourself if you would feel happier and more fulfilled if you found ways to make useful contributions to your fellow beings. Reflect on what you have read in this chapter and then refer to the personal reflections you wrote in your journal. Ask yourself if you can incorporate these choices into your life and as you journal your thoughts keep in mind the following pearl of wisdom:

Right Now I Am One Choice Away From A New Beginning

35. Metaphors you live by

The greatest thing in style is to have a command of metaphor.

—Aristotle

We often communicate with ourselves and others with metaphors. As the old saying goes, a picture is worth a thousand words. The same can be said about metaphors. They are short cuts in communication that allow us to explain complex inner experiences. Because metaphors are so powerful, we need to choose them wisely and consciously. The metaphors we live by will enhance or destroy our experience of peace and joy in life.

It is important to emphasize that not only do metaphors reflect our current life and experiences; they also create our life and experiences. You may be wondering what this means. An example may clarify. If you say to yourself that "My life is like a tornado", likely is short hand for communicating that your life is chaotic and overwhelming. Think about how different it would be to communicate to yourself that "Life is a precious gift" or "Life is a rat race", or "Life is a game".

One way to create extraordinarily rapid changes in your experience is to be more mindful of the words and the metaphors you use when you communicate with yourself or others. Think about the metaphors you live by that have an empowering or disempowering impact on your life. Think about the metaphors you use about yourself, other people, the world, life and the future.

Think about how challenging life would be if you lived by the following metaphors:

I am a disaster magnet.

Others are vultures.

The world is going to hell in a hand basket.

Life is battle.

The future is a black hole.

You would probably agree that life would be quite painful, and devoid of peace, if you lived by these metaphors. It would also have a way of creating experiences in line with these disempowering metaphors. As the father of motivation, Earl Nightingale was know to say, "We become what we think about most of the time". Our thoughts, which include metaphors, do contribute to the outcomes and experiences we create in our life. The good news is; we are in the drivers seat when it comes to controlling our thoughts (did you catch the metaphor?).

Spend some time choosing the metaphors that you wish to guide your life, relationships and experiences. What metaphors will cultivate a life of peace and joy?

Daily Practices

Day One: Identify one metaphor that you have used to describe YOURSELF. Write it down. Is this metaphor empowering or disempowering? Does this metaphor create personal peace for you, or block you from experiencing peace and joy? If the metaphor you identified is disempowering, identify an empowering alternative.

Day Two: Identify one metaphor that you have used to describe OTHER PEOPLE. Write it down. Is this metaphor empowering or disempowering? Does this metaphor create personal peace for you, or block you from experiencing peace and joy? If the metaphor you identified is disempowering, identify an empowering alternative.

Day Three: Identify one metaphor that you have used to describe THE WORLD. Write it down. Is this metaphor empowering or disempowering? Does this metaphor create personal peace for you, or block you from experiencing peace and joy? If the metaphor you identified is disempowering, identify an empowering alternative.

Day Four: Identify one metaphor that you have used to describe LIFE. Write it down. Is this metaphor empowering or disempowering? Does this metaphor create personal peace for you, or block you from experiencing peace and joy? If the metaphor you identified is disempowering, identify an empowering alternative.

Day Five: Identify one metaphor that you have used to describe THE FUTURE. Write it down. Is this metaphor empowering or disempowering? Does this metaphor create personal peace for you, or block you from experiencing peace and joy? If the metaphor you identified is disempowering, identify an empowering alternative.

Day Six: Write out each of the empowering metaphors that you identified. Put them in the order of:

> I am...
> Others are...

The world is…
Life is…
The future is…

Repeat these metaphors several times out loud. State them with passion and with a feeling of certainty that you already are enjoying the rewards of abundance and personal peace from living your life out of these empowering metaphors.

Day Seven: Read your empowering metaphors several times out loud with passion and certainty. Use your journal to write about what kind of life you would create if you allowed these metaphors to guide you.

Dr. Mike Davison, Kay Guzder

36. Keep your eye on the prize

"You become what you think about."

—Earl Nightingale

"Focus on where you want to go, not on what you fear."

—Anthony Robbins

Goal setting is foundational to any personal or spiritual journey. In the words of Stephen Covey, it helps you begin with the end in mind. Without goals, life seems to just happen. Circumstances seem to control you and you often find yourself in reaction mode.

Some of the basics of goal setting include writing down your goals. Many research studies show that only 3 percent of the population actually writes down goals. And only a fraction of this 3 percent review their goals on a consist basis. You deserve to be in this small elite group.

I have heard genius be described as the "ability to focus on one thing at a time." Many people who are "geniuses" are so not only because they have a high intellect, but also because they have a gift of being able to focus on the objective or goal at hand.

This same focus must come in to play when determining what your goals are in relation to success. You need to learn to work towards one major objective and juggle a few short- and mid-range goals at the same time.

One way to determine what your direction is (and ultimately what your goals are) is to do a check-up. We suggest listing 7 categories: Financial, Career, Family, Personal, Spiritual, Mental, and Physical. Rank your goals in these categories and how you're doing. This will illustrate to you where you are and where you would like to be and exactly how balanced you are as you move toward your desired outcomes.

* Set goals that are smart. Big goals must be broken down into manageable steps. Don't set more than 4 goals to work on during a single day. Seek divine guidance and direction on each goal.

* Identify what the pay-off is when you achieve your goal. Nebulous rewards don't motivate people to achieve much.

* List the obstacles that stand between you and your goals. If you are not aware of potential problems, you'll be side-tracked when they arise and you may lose sight of your objective.

* Have someone in your corner who can dispense counsel and guidance.

* Think about who can help you achieve your goal. Identify friends who can be encouragers and who can help keep you motivated and on-track.

* List the skills and knowledge required to attain your goal.

* Develop a plan of action to achieve your goal

* Set a deadline for achievement. It is hard to achieve

something that has no ending date.

As you consider your goals, ask yourself the following questions:

* ✳ Is this really my goal?

* ✳ Is this morally right and fair to everyone involved?

* ✳ Will it take me closer to my long-range goal?

* ✳ Can I commit myself to start and reach this objective?

* ✳ Can I see myself attaining this goal?

You should answer yes to each of these questions. If not, re-evaluate!

And then give each goal a final test of the "basic wants" in life:

* ✳ Will it make me happier?

* ✳ Will it make me healthier?

* ✳ Will it make me more prosperous?

* ✳ Will it increase my security?

* ✳ Will it help me make more friends?

* ✳ Will it give me peace of mind?

* ✳ Will it improve my family (and other) relationships?

* ✳ Will it increase my hope for the future?

If you can't answer yes to each of these questions, re-evaluate your goal.

Daily Practices

Day One: First identify what is most important in the below CATEGORIES of your life. Do this in one to three sentences. Think precisely. Think concretely. In other words, use language that would allow you to objectively evaluate if you have accomplished your desired outcomes.

Intimate relationship:

Friendships:

Health:

Career:

Finances:

Recreation:

Spirituality:

Day Two: Rate your level of satisfaction with each category of your life. Use something simple such as 1) Not at all satisfied 2) Somewhat satisfied 3) Very Satisfied

Intimate relationship: (Rating ___)

Friendships: (Rating ___)

Health: (Rating ___)

Career: (Rating ___)

Finances: (Rating ___)

Recreation: (Rating ___)

Spirituality: (Rating ___)

Day Three: Answer the following questions as completely as you are able.

1. Identify the category where you feel you want most to change RIGHT NOW.

2. What do you most want in this category? (STATE IN POSITIVE TERMS)

3. What will that change do for you, when you have achieved it? (Think about WHY this goal(s) is important to you).

4. What control do you have over getting what you want? (Do you have sufficient control?)

5. How will you know when you have it? (Be extremely specific. For example, what will you see, hear, and feel? What will you be doing? How would you be thinking about yourself, other people, and the future? when you have what you want?)

6. Where, when and with who do you want to share this with?

Day Four: Answer the following questions as completely as you are able.

How will accomplishing this goal affect the remaining categories of your life? (Intended and unintended ways as well)

What resources do you already have that will contribute to getting what you want? These resources can be internal or external.

Example of INTERNAL RESOURCE: Flexibility, persistence, etc…

Example of EXTERNAL RESOURCE: Books, friends, coach, mentor, etc…

What additional resources do you need in order to get to what you want? Again, include internal and external resources.

Day Five: Answer the following questions as completely as you are able.

How are you going to get "there"? (Identify the specific action steps you will take)

As you look at what it will take to get your goal, is it worthwhile?

What would it mean to you if you did not accomplish this desired outcome?

Day Six: Share your responses to this week's practices with a trusted person. Ask them to tune in on the following:

Where did you sense the most energy?

What insights and or patterns do you see?

Do you think you have sufficient control over the outcome?

Where do you need to be more specific?

What additional information is needed to completely understand where you are going and how you will get there?

What ideas do you have for me?

What challenges do you see for me?

Day Seven: Review your practices from this week. Identify specific action steps you will take based on the practices over the past week. Remember, SELF-EXAMINATION is the breakfast of champions, FEEDBACK is the lunch of champions, ACTION is the dinner of champions, and CELEBRATING YOUR SUCCESSES is the evening snack of champions.

37. Cultivate your talents and unique abilities

"I believe that every person is born with talent."

—Maya Angelou

I believe that we are all geniuses, just different kinds. It saddens me when someone goes through life and does not allow themself to foster and develop their God-given abilities. Do you know what yours are? It may have vocational implications and maybe it doesn't. However, I feel that one of our obligations while on this planet is to figure out our talents and cultivate them. Maybe it is to teach or preach, to write or speak, to be an amazing caretaker, to be an extraordinary parent. The list is endless. What ever your unique talents are, you will experience a greater sense of personal peace when you cultivate them and use them in the service of the greater good.

I want to pose a challenge. That challenge is to look at it as your ethical imperative to develop your unique abilities and to see it as your obligation to the world and your creator. Remember a talent is not a talent unless you discover it and make use of it in a positive way to contribute to the world.

What good would Michael Jordan's talent in athletics have been if he chose to be a beer guzzling coach potato? Now I am not taking anything away from Michael Jordan or anyone else. The potential for the talent is there. The rest is up to you. I have heard many stories about Michael Jordan's work ethic regarding basketball. He worked harder than anyone and had higher standards for himself than anyone else. I don't know if he viewed cultivating his talent as a way of honoring God and contributing to the world, but I believe it did both.

Also regarding your unique abilities and talents, they must continually be developed and refined. I believe that a special talent can become rather flat or stale if not continually honed. Stephen Covey referred to it as sharpening the saw.

Cultivating your unique abilities also requires being aware of your less developed areas. As Socrates said, "Know thy self". If you have underdeveloped areas, be aware of how they could get in the way of fully expressing your unique abilities. I know a brilliant research engineer that is underdeveloped in his communications skills. This has made him less successful at getting his inventions to market. Regarding the less developed areas it is important to learn strategies to bypass them, use your strengths to catapult over them or collaborate with others with different and compatible talents and skills.

Connecting with your spiritual gift requires digging deeper into your own self on your own or with the help of others. It is about figuring out what lies at the root of your peak experiences and/or times when you felt deeply satisfied with who you are and what you are doing. Don't narrowly focus on things such as your job title. Focus more on roles (work and non-work related) that draw as much as possible on your unique talents. That is the key to personal and professional fulfillment.

Daily Practices

Day One: Using your journal, identify your accomplishments for which you are most proud.

Day Two: Use your journal to contemplate these questions:

I feel most alive (or at home) when I am (doing)…

I love to advise other about…

I feel most energized when…

Day Three: Use your journal to contemplate these questions:

What I find myself almost obsessed about is…

I frequently day dream about…

Day Four: Use your journal to contemplate these questions:

Unique life experiences I have had…

What outrages me…

What have I overcome in life…

Day Five: Use your journal to contemplate these questions:

What seems to come easy to me that other people struggle with…

People always compliment me about…

Day Six: Interview at least three people today—you can use the phone, email, or in person. Try to use people who know you well and ideally people who know you from different contexts (home, community, work, etc…). Also use people who are going to be absolutely honest with you. Ask your interviewees what they see as your unique abilities, talents, strengths or spiritual gift. Prime the people about different areas where they think you excel. Some broad domains include: career, relationships, communication, professionalism, organization, overcoming challenges, style, outlook, attitude, and overall skill sets.

Day Seven: Based on the amazing journey into your spiritual gifts write a summary of what you feel are your greatest gifts and how you can use them to impact the world in your own unique way.

38. Visualizing: Make your dreams a reality

"There is a law in psychology that if you form a picture in your mind of what you would like to be, and you keep and hold that picture there long enough, you will soon become exactly as you have been thinking."

—William James

A few years ago I became acquainted with a unique boarding school located in the mountains above San Bernardino, California called The CEDU School. It specialized in helping teens and young adolescents who had become disenfranchised and discouraged. One of the first things that occurred when new students were admitted to the school was that all brand name vanity clothes were confiscated by the staff and given to the parents to take home. Items such as jackets depicting gang symbols, clothing picturing famous rock stars, even clothing with major league sports team logos or player's names and numbers on them were taken away. As this was a residential school where the students live on average a couple of years before they graduate, the teenagers would not be seeing these items again for a long time. You can imagine the uproar at the first student assembly as these were being collected. These items had become a symbol for a false identity these teens had chosen. It was their sense of power and uniqueness and had displaced their sense of self.

In enforcing this rule the school began to teach the important lesson that no one derives useful personal strength and talent by borrowing an identity from someone else. By attaching their identities to the status symbols of commercial products and superstars, the young people gave away an important part of themselves—their personal power and sense of self. How could they develop a sense of confidence in themselves if they were so dependent on projecting their image as some superstar, sports hero or gang member? As a matter of fact, in the case of these students, such status symbols robbed them of the chance to develop their own sense of identity and personal self worth. Relying on symbols to gain an identity, whether it is sports, gang, or brand related, is an empty gesture that interferes with the process of identifying your own personal strengths and talents.

After the dreaded purging of the status symbols, the new CEDU students were met by faculty members who explained why this was a hard and fast rule of the school. The students were given the new dress code they would be wearing for the duration of their stay and the faculty launched right into a lecture on the history and principles of the founding father of the school. They were introduced to new symbols and guiding mottos that would become the roadmaps and mainstays of their journey toward emotional growth, maturity, self worth and self confidence.

While at CEDU, the student attended classes in the academic subjects, but even more emphasis was placed on teaching the emotional and social skills needed to live and thrive in society. Notice here the key word is *thrive*. They were taught not just how to survive, but how to thrive. They learned to respect and rely on themselves. They were taught to make a contribution and to reach out to others and lend a helping hand. They learned to cooperate when faced with daunting tasks. They found their courage and learned to value teamwork. They got to know themselves and what brought meaning to their lives, rather than hiding behind the empty slogans, ad campaigns and hype of superstardom.

It is difficult to capture the attention of teenagers and the new students at CEDU were no exception. They were restless in that first assembly as they listened to the story of how CEDU began in the vision of a man who saw a gathering of troubled teens and took action to bring about change. One evening as he and his wife sat on their front porch he noticed a group of youngsters gathering and milling about a teen hangout across the street from their home. After observing them for several evenings, he recognized that something unhealthy was going on. The young people seemed to be adrift and were engaging in dangerous activities. He decided to invite them to his home for an evening of soft drinks, snacks and conversation. He asked his wife to help him make the young people feel welcome. They decided on a few house rules, namely no one could come into their home under the influence of drugs or alcohol and there would be no vandalizing of the property. The first evening five young people came to the gathering, the next night the number doubled and that number continued to increase each week until the house was filled every night. As the evening socials continued the couple got to know the youngsters. They gained their trust and got them talking about their struggles and conflicts. They were trying to help these young people find their direction and sense of worth. They asked them to see who they were and what they could do with it.

One day as the couple drove away from their home they noticed someone had spray painted the word CEDU on their mailbox. Thinking they had been vandalized, they asked those gathered that evening what happened and who was responsible. They were surprised by the proud response of one young man who volunteered that he had written the letters on the mailbox. He was most sincere about his artwork and not at all apologetic. He explained that he felt transformed early on by the idea presented by the couple to "see who you are and what you can do with it." For this young man the symbol SEE/DO translated into CEDU. It became his motto for finding and redirecting himself away from a wasted life. He was enthusiastic and wanted others to come to the meetings to "see who they were and what they could do." The young man explained what a turning point it was for him when he realized that he could make choices in his life and not just drift along wherever the tide took him. Others picked up on this motto and the founder of the school took the opportunity that night to teach the group how to begin to create a new vision of who they were and what they wanted to do with their lives. The CEDU Group became the new name for the gathering from then on.

From this seed a dream was born and the founders turned their talents of salesmanship into mentoring young people. The man who originally formed the group was not a trained counselor. He and his wife owned a furniture store and he was trained in sales and business. The group also transformed his life. He decided to take members of the CEDU group with him as he searched for some property in the mountains above his home in San Bernadino. He wanted to expand on his rapidly growing vision of a permanent location for a school to help disenfranchised adolescents. Eventually, he discovered an old abandoned hunting lodge that once belonged to the Hollywood producer, John

Huston's, grandfather. Wealthy film moguls had used it as a gathering place when they were hunting game but it had been closed and was for sale. CEDU's founder made inquiries and identified sponsors. He was able to make his dream a reality when he bought the property to start his school. The teens were given the task of repairing the dilapidated buildings, mixing and pouring cement walkways and laying out the plans for paving a basketball court and a parking lot. Next the professional staff and faculty were hired and the CEDU School was born, his vision became a reality.

This story began back in the 1960's with the dropout hippy population surging and the vision of one man who knew it could be different. Since then the school has graduated hundreds of students who have gone on to schools of higher education throughout the country. At CEDU these young people unburdened themselves by discarding their negative habits and paralyzing self doubts. They learned how to visualize a dream for themselves and their lives. They learned to take some small steps and then the giant leaps it took to make their dreams dome true. Some of them went on to realize big dreams by going to medical school. Others attained their professional degrees from well known universities and schools of higher education. Some reached out and made their dreams come true by using their talents to create successful businesses and make a contribution to their community. Many of them returned to The CEDU School as counselors and teachers who wanted to help other youngsters find and fulfill their dreams. They wanted to give something back to the school that had given so much to them.

I personally know one special young man who did a lot of soul searching on the basketball court at CEDU. He found himself, his talent and his self worth. He had a dream of attending the University of Arizona in Tucson, the home of his all time favorite basketball team. He worked very hard to get admitted and is now in his senior year. He will be graduating soon and in my opinion he has already achieved a great deal of success. I wish him well in his next adventure.

Perhaps you can identify with some of the feelings these teens had as they arrived at CEDU. Maybe there have been times in your life that you have felt lost, frustrated, or stuck in self defeating behaviors. Maybe you have tried to hide behind a false identity so that others would accept you not as you are, but as you pretend to be. Let today be your first day of school as you visualize yourself as an adolescent learning to find your authentic identity. Seek the courage to believe in yourself and create a life in which you come to know your unique gifts and use them to your advantage and in service to others. Let your imagination flow, let your ideas come forth and have the courage to give yourself permission to explore *"Who you are and what you can do with it."*

Daily Practices

Day One: Spend some time journaling about how you hide your true identity from others. Visualize this false self and reflect on what it is that you fear about living authentically.

Day Two: Spend some time journaling about who you are. Send your false self away and get in touch with your real self. Make a list of the positive things you know about yourself. As well, make a list of the things you don't feel good about when you look inward. The point of doing this is to celebrate the wonderful things about yourself, and to generate a list of the things you want to change about yourself

Dr. Mike Davison, Kay Guzder

Day Three: Write a paragraph for the "School Yearbook" about yourself. Write an authentic statement about who you are, what your interests are and what you want to be when you grow up.

Day Four: Spend some time journaling about your life and "What you want to do with it."

Day Five: Spend some time journaling about the hurdles you will need to leap over to make your vision of yourself and your life a reality. Hurdles are the ways you block yourself from living your life authentically. They can be internal, such as a belief that you can't try things because you might fail or get rejected. They can be external, such as finding a way to finance college tuition or start a new business.

Day Six: Spend some time reflecting and journaling about what your vision is for yourself in the next five years. How do you want to grow internally?

Day Seven: Read your journal entry from yesterday and ask yourself how you can begin to live your life in a way that reflects your authentic self. What steps can you take to make your vision a reality and make your dreams come true? Write your ideas and dreams in your journal.

> "We should be taught not to wait for inspiration to start a thing. Action always generates inspiration. Inspiration seldom generates action."
>
> —*Frank Tibolt*

Section VI. Relationships of Peace

39. Reconciling anger to create peace in life

"Let us not look back in anger or forward with fear but around in awareness."

—James Thurber

I'M SO ANGRY...

"I just can't sleep! I keep replaying and rehashing the same situation over and over in my head and it's driving me crazy!"

"Man, just you wait until I get my chance, I'll show them. I'll get them twice as bad as they got me!"

"I'm so mad but there is nothing I can do about it. I can't even talk about it. I feel so hurt and betrayed. I'm holding it all inside. I feel like I'm getting an ulcer."

"I'm totally frustrated! My jaw is sore from grinding my teeth. I can't get rid of these angry feelings. I'm so depressed."

"I'm so angry I want to punch someone or something. They asked for it and they're going to get it!"

I've heard these above quotes as people expressed the feelings of anger that were overwhelming them. We all experience feelings of anger and many times these feelings are passionate, intense and they leave us reeling. Think about red hot anger, the kind that jumps up, grabs hold and spins you around into a response of overreaction. Think about the slow simmering type of anger that begins with small irritating bubbles and builds for days until it becomes a boiling cauldron of rage that explodes Then there's that sneaky "somehow I've been betrayed" anger. How about the "you broke your promise and my heart, I'll never trust anyone again and I'm going to punish everyone" type of anger?

The most dangerous anger is the extreme type the gets acted out as a total loss of control that leads to verbal and physical violence and even murder. Often this type of anger is accompanied by a justification that the victim was responsible because, "they made me do it by making me so mad." Madness is the key word here.

It is common knowledge that anger impacts us physically as well as emotionally whether it is expressed outwardly as in violent outbursts or held inwardly where it impacts the immune system and can causes system wide physical damage.

While the above examples and symptoms may have some familiarity, you might not be aware of the futility attached to feelings of anger when they are expressed outwardly or "kept in a gunny sack" internally to be revisited endlessly. Angry feelings normally have a certain sense of futility and defeat attached to them because they are so emotionally charged. At some level we know we are acting irrationally because we recognize that a sensitive chord has been struck that makes us respond so strongly. Anger, more often than not, arises from one of two sources. We either feel we're getting something we don't want, such as being over controlled, humiliated, insulted or demeaned, or we feel we're not getting something we want, like respect, love, affection, attention or recognition. Most people first learn about ways anger gets expressed in their family of origin. Those that are not taught how to deal with the strong emotion of anger either learn to turn their angry feelings inward and not express them or to express anger outward and take it out on others by becoming an aggressive bully. Sometimes this bullying takes on a subtle form and becomes a passive aggressive stance. These negative tactics never work well and they don't contribute to developing and maintaining healthy relationships. When dealing with the problem of anger across such a widespread and diverse set of circumstances, it is helpful to have some tools that will get you out of the win/lose arenas that keep you endlessly spinning your wheels and sparring over the same issues repeatedly.

In his book entitled, Anger, Wisdom for Cooling the Flames, author, poet, peace activist, and Nobel Peace Prize Nominee, Thich Nhat Hanh, suggests specific techniques for handling and re-channeling anger. His teachings incorporate the use of meditation and deep breathing techniques which call upon us to acknowledge our anger and think about its source. This approach allows us to slow down the process until we can clear our minds to think rationally how to resolve our anger with a cool head and clear mind. He does not ask us to dismiss the source of our conflict but to bring it into a clearer focus. Thich Nhat Hanh suggests that we deal with the issues related to our anger in the present moment. This technique allows us to deal directly and clearly with the source of our anger and keeps us away from the distractions of past history and future expectations. Neither visiting past history nor jumping into the future is useful when dealing with the present conflict. It only causes confusion. The benefit of staying in the present moment is to be able to assess the situation with clarity, take stock of what is really going on, think through the situation, and then make rational decisions about how to resolve the conflict. We may not always get the outcome we want but we learn that we have many choices when we are trying to respond to conflict and anger. We also learn we don't have to take responsibility for anger directed at us from others and remain a victim without resources. Thich Nhat Hanh's method of using breathing techniques, staying in the present moment and keeping peace in your heart when dealing with feelings of anger, are potent formulas for incorporating permanent changes that bring lasting results in the ways you can manage your anger.

The benefit of applying these approaches to anger management and conflict resolution is to experience the power of disarming inflammatory situations. By listening to the other side of the conflict and stating your needs clearly, solutions can be found that are not possible when each person's goal is to defeat the other. By approaching each conflict while keeping peace in your heart, you decide to live your life harmoniously. This is a choice and most people are not aware they have this option. If you let people know you intend to live your life in harmony and keep hostile and aggressive emotions away from your environment you will give a strong message that goes a long way toward empowering yourself in any conflictual situation. It is a powerful means of disarming and discharging your anger and the anger of others.

Recently I read a sign in front of a local church that I feel offered a great deal of wisdom. It read:

IF YOU LOSE YOUR TEMPER,
DON'T GO LOOKING FOR IT!

Daily Practices

Day One: Spend some time reflecting and journaling about what you learned in your family of origin about expressing anger. Write as much as you wish on this topic, either a few paragraphs or an epiphany if you wish.

Day Two: Spend some time reflecting and identifying the feelings that are most familiar to you when you are embroiled in an angry encounter. For example: I am desperate to control this situation; I am determined to win no matter what the cost; I want to attack, I want to avoid the conflict, I just want it to go away; I am just going to give in; I'll give in but then feel resentful and I'll punish at a later time; I'm just going to stay silent and I'm not going to give in.

These are just a few examples. Write your own personal examples in your journal and then try to identify what physical symptoms you feel in response to your anger. Ask yourself how your anger is affecting you? Ask yourself where you are feeling your anger in your body? Where are you carrying that anger? Write in your journal about the physical consequences of unresolved anger to your health.

Day Three: Spend some time journaling about how well your old ways of expressing anger work for you. Do you get what you want and feel effective in the way you react when you are upset, or do you feel frustrated and misunderstood after engaging in a conflicted situation?

Day Four: Spend some time journaling about ways that you can choose to deal with anger effectively and maintain your composure while showing respect for the position of those you disagree with.

Day Five: Spend some time reflecting on one issue about anger that is particularly troubling to you. Decide how you want to respond by choosing one of the new ways of responding that you have learned. Write in your journal about how you want to proceed toward reaching a resolution.

Day Six: Spend some time journaling about mistakes you have made in angry encounters in the past. Think about what changes you want to in handling your anger in future conflicts. Honestly incorporate the methods you use in conflict situations and take a look at whether you "fan the flames" of your anger or withdraw and avoid dealing with it at all. Ask yourself if you let your anger grow until it becomes explosive. Ask if you are internalizing your anger into silent rage?.

Day Seven: Spend some time meditating and visualizing yourself in a situation where you are seriously angry. Imagine yourself responding in ways that result in feeling in charge of your emotions and expressing your position calmly. Picture yourself managing your anger, focusing on resolution and not victimizing others or becoming a victim. Write a few paragraphs in your journal about what you visualized and how you felt as you pictured yourself taking part in this conflicted situation.

40. The myth of the self made person

No man is an island, entire of itself; every man is a piece of the continent, a part of the main; if a clod be washed away by the sea, Europe is the less...any man's death diminishes me, because I am involved in mankind...

—John Donne

Somewhere on your road to spiritual fulfillment and peace of mind, you will begin to understand that you are really never alone. There are amazing sources of strength and help everywhere you look. You will have to look to find them and then know how to use them.

Having a "team" is incredibly important as you walk along your path. You may reap the benefits of success in your world, but you won't get there alone. The fallacy of the "self-made person" is just that—a fallacy. Everyone is influenced directly and indirectly by scores of people. Let's look at a list of the teams that each of us can access.

※ Parents: if they were there to raise you, they had the greatest influence on your life. Feelings of love and security are established early—as early as birth. Children who have parents who love, care for, and protect them gain enormously both psychologically and physiologically.

✱ Teachers: chances are there is a teacher who has made an impression on you that you remember to this day. Positive or negative, there are teachers in our lives who have the power to mold us and shape us. Sometimes we choose paths in response to a negative example a teacher has left us; more often than not, we choose paths that are due to the positive influence they've left in our lives.

✱ Friends: the happiest and most successful people tend to have a wide range of friends from different walks of life. Friends encourage us, lift us up, and are part of an inextricable support system in our lives.

✱ Mentors: smart people who truly desire success find mentors that will walk with them as they traverse their road. Mentors can point out pitfalls and potholes in the road that we might otherwise miss, and their experience and willingness to teach us is an invaluable gift.

✱ Spiritual Leaders: ministers, priests, rabbis, pastors, etc., are in an amazing position to contribute positively and significantly in your life. Their ability to see beyond the current circumstances and share life and light is unparalleled. Having a spiritual leader doesn't guarantee that you'll never feel despair, but it does guarantee that you won't have to go through the dark times alone.

Just as you have a team as you work towards further actualizing your self, you can be a part of someone else's team as well. Be a friend to someone who is just starting out on their own journey—encourage them, mentor them (if appropriate), and commit to be there for them when they need you. Do the right thing (remember your integrity), and have compassion in all situations. As you build your team your ability to develop yourself psychologically and spiritually will also expand.

Daily Practices

One of the keys to a happy and spiritually fulfilling life is the ability to have great relationships—at home, at work, and in your social life. This week's practices will help you further develop the necessary skills that will help your deepen your relationships. Remember to use your journal, be playful and take action. Have a spirit of willingness to experiment.

Day One: Being a good listener is a key to a deep connection with another person. Today go out of your way to show a sincere interest in what is happening in someone else's life. Remember that we have one mouth but two ears. In essence, you should be doing twice as much listening as talking.

Day Two: Being able to put yourself in the other person's shoes is another key to having a deep connection with another person. Today, focus on seeing things from someone else' perspective. Today, when listening to someone momentarily step into their world. Being in the other person's world requires that you listen with openess. In other words, while you are listening you do that and only that—you listen.

Day Three: Look for the other people's strengths, talents, and virtues. Everyone has strengths and you have a choice in whether you pay more attention to their good points or their imperfections. The more you discover a person's good points and focus on these the more your respect for them increases. Today identify three strengths of at least three people you have regular contact with. This will be especially helpful if you have having challenges in a relationship with any specific individual.

Day Four: Keep in touch with others. Is there an important person in your life who you have not connected with recently? Maybe it is due to time or geography. Relationships need nourishment to be sustained. Even long-distance relationships can endure for decades if they are nourished. Today write a letter, send a card, make a call or email at least one person to nourish the relationship.

Day Five: Earlier this week we focused on understanding other people's perspective; to be able to see the world from their viewpoint. An extension of this is to RESPECT the other person's perspective. It is important to be mindful that many of us see things very differently. We all have a different working model of the world in our heads. Learning to embrace the idea that we can transcend the perspective of someone having to be "right" and someone having to be "wrong". Identify a time where you recently had a difference of opinion with someone else and you got caught up in having to defend your "rightness" or convince them of their "wrongness". What were the consequences to the relationship? How could you have been more respectful and accepting of their perspective?

Day Six: Extending yesterday's practice, think of how you can be more accepting and respectful of other people's imperfections. From a position of humility, "weaknesses" are best understood as our own subjective evaluations based on our own working model of the world or the way things should be.

Day Seven: Part of respecting and accepting others includes not trying to change people. Appreciate who they are, not what you perceive as their potential. Identify in your journal how you have tried to change other people. Remember, unsolicited advice is typically not well received. Identify how you can be more excepting of what you perceive to be other people's imperfections or differing worldviews.

41. Reflection on family

When our relatives are at home, we have to think of all their good points or it would be impossible to endure them.

—George Bernard Shaw

Once you know the formula for spiritual fulfillment and success, it is time to consider different avenues in which that formula should be put in to action. The main one you will find in every area of your life is relationships. Quality relationships are key to cultivating personal peace.

Why relationships? Because we are human beings, designed to interact with other human beings. This, by default, entails relationships. And also, by default, if you don't have appropriate skills to manage your relationships, you will likely feel a great sense of disconnection and lack even a basic feeling of contentment.

Before getting to your family relationships, the first relationship you must consider is the one you have with yourself. If you don't like yourself, chances are great you will project that dislike to others and your lack of self-appreciation will not propel you to a feeling of peace of mind. The higher your integrity is, the more you will like yourself. The more you like yourself, the better your relationships will be with others.

Your family relationships are also very import to examine. The most successful Harvard Business graduates (class of 1949, by percentages) had several things in common:

✻ they had wives who supported their work and endeavors; women who were intelligent and able to share ideas and be a sounding board (Clearly it works both ways, but this powerful study was done in 1949).

✻ they built their personal, family, and business lives on a foundation of integrity.

Family relationships are extremely important as you consider your path to spiritual fulfillment. If you fail here, you will not succeed elsewhere. You will not achieve the peace of mind you deserve.

Think about how you can turn your home into a sanctuary. Creating your home as a sanctuary means creating an environment where you can live moment-to-moment with a greater level of awareness and intentionality. This kind of active presence is cultivated by refining your capacity to pay attention, sustain that attention over time, and be fully present in your home and for your family.

Participating in relationships in a fuller way allows us to be more present, thus allowing us others to be who they truly are. This allows us to more frequently act with a greater degree of wisdom and compassion. The more we are able to keep in mind the wholeness and beauty of others (especially in those difficult times) the more our ability to be deeply connected with others increases.

Remember...

There are very few people who, on their deathbeds, proclaim "I wish I'd spent more time at the office." I think a lot of people reflect back on how connected they were with their family.

Be careful...

You don't want to be on your rocking chair reflecting back and feel that you did not bring enough perspective to your home and your family. Figure out what you need to do to avoid being too economically focused, or too stressed. While matters such as economics do need to be part of your focus, it is about balance.

Live your life in a SUSTAINABLE way.

Here are some daily practices to help you be more present in your home and more focused on what is most important to you.

Daily Practices

Day One: There is a debate in some circles about quality versus quantity of time spent with your loved ones. The more important point that they are both important and should be maintained to keep developing and maintaining deep connections.

> **Exercise:** Think about the last month. How have you done in the area of "quality of time" and "quantity of time" that you have spent with your family? Have you put in the time and been fully present in your interactions with your loved ones? Remember, you can't improve upon that which you don't acknowledge.

Day Two: Focus on seeing things from your family member's point of view. This involves purposefully, and willingly suspending your own ideas or perspective.

A client of mine recently shared the following results when doing this exercise. She stated that; "My seven-year-old son was talking back to my husband and I. I later realized that he was upset when my husband and I were having a date night. "I don't want to eat this slop!" he yelled at dinnertime. However, when I stepped back and saw things from his perspective... I realized that my son was jealous, and therefore speaking irrationally. Seeing things from my son's perspective helps me to not to overreact to his behavior.

> **Exercise:** Spend a few moments today stepping into a family member's point of view. Image how he or she experiences the world and what is most important for them.

Day Three: Imagine how you appear and sound and are experienced from the point of view of your loved ones.

> **Exercise:** Spend a moment today in your imagination experiencing what it would be like to be in a relationship with yourself. In other words, how do others likely experience you? More specifically, how do you carry yourself, how do you speak, what you say, what emotions do you evoke in others.

Day Four: Get clear about the expectations you have for your loved ones. How do you communicate those expectations?

> **Exercise:** Spend a moment reflecting on the expectations you have for your loved ones. Are they healthy and reasonable? Do you communicate your expectations in a clear, direct and loving manner?

Day Five: Apologize to your family and/or loved ones when you have fallen short, even in a small way. Acknowledging your behavior and making amends is nurturing and healing in relationships, they demonstrate that you understand your impact on them and you deeply care about their needs and feelings.

> **Specific Exercise:** Think about if there are recent behaviors you need to acknowledge and make amends for. Identify a plan and a time line to have this important conversation.

Day Six: Use your journal to identify the strengths and weaknesses of each of your important relationships.

Day Seven: Use your journal and identify one thing you can do to improve your most important relationships. Remember small things can make a big difference, particularly if you are consistent.

42. Opening up

What is true is already so.
Owning up to it doesn't make it worse.
Not being open about it doesn't make it go away.
And because it's true, it is what is there to be interacted with.
Anything untrue isn't there to be lived.
People can stand what is true,
for they are already enduring it.

—Eugene Gendlin

How much do you participate in your relationships? I have a young male client at this time who openly acknowledged to me today that the most he ever participates in his relationships is 40%. By that he means only 40% of who he is, is known by others. He is able to identify that his tendency to play it safe by keeping others at a safe distance is connected to the death of his mother early in his life. While he understands it, his isolation perpetuates his pain and feeling of disconnection from others.

This young man clearly sees that there is a connection between his lack of participation in relationships and his emotional problems. He sees that the roadblock to participating more fully in relationships is fear of rejection, feelings

Dr. Mike Davison, Kay Guzder

of inadequacy, shame, and the potential of abandonment. Opening ourselves up to others does involve risk. At the same time a true sense of personal peace is only possible when we have an intimate circle in which we can be transparent.

You may be able to identify in some way with the challenge of the young man mentioned above. Are there aspects of who you are, or parts of your personal history that you have held back from people in your most intimate circle? What has blocked you from being more open? Not to sound trite, but the saying "The only way out is through" is true. Translated, the only way to transcend the self-centered emotions of fear of rejection, inadequacy, shame, and fear of abandonment are to show up more fully in relationships. Opening up and engaging more fully in relationships is good for your emotional, spiritual and physical health.

The theme of deeper involvement with others is emphasized throughout psychological and spiritual literature. The language used to describe this process may be different in various contexts. It may be referred to as being more of who you are, being authentic, opening up, confessing or countless other ways. From my perspective, it doesn't matter what you call it. Deep involvement and deeper disclosure is good for all aspects of your emotional, physical, spiritual and relational health. In the medical and psychology literature there are countless studies that validate this notion.

Within the major spiritual traditions the benefits of opening up are emphasized. In the Christian tradition, the value of confession is emphasized as a way of deepening one's relationship with God and reducing emotions such as guilt. Guilt is fueled by secrecy. Guilt is counter to personal peace and leaves us feeling separated from ourselves, God, and others. We all know on some level the negative emotional and physical consequences of guilt.

Within the Jewish tradition, Yom Kippur is the Day of Atonement. This is a day that is devoted to confessional practices to achieve restitution and ultimately deepen one's relationship with God.

Within the Buddhist tradition, author Pema Chodron described the process and benefit of confession. The process of opening up leads to a spiritual cleansing, which allows an individual to transcend repetitive unfinished patterns of thinking, feeling and/or behaving.

The aspects of self or past behavior which we feel shameful about continues to have a way of running us if we continue to resist openly acknowledging them. I have heard it said many times, "that which we resist, persists".

I have also seen the emotional, physical and spiritual benefits of "opening up" for individuals (from different faith traditions) with drug, alcohol or other addictive problems who participate in 12 step programs. In 12 step programs there is also an emphasis on moving toward a greater experience of connection with God and others through the process of disclosure and sharing. In one of the steps, members as asked to conduct a "fearless moral inventory". In another step it is suggested that members take that inventory and share it with "God, ourselves and another human being..." There are later steps, which involve cleaning up past messes, repairing damaged relationships (with oneself and others) and conducting daily inventories and promptly acknowledging when one does wrong. I have seen amazing transformation occur within individuals who practice these principles at deep levels. They experience a greater connection with themselves, God and others, and as a result enjoy profound emotional and physical benefits.

This week's daily practices will be focused on helping you identify what you have not been completely open and honest about. Please use your journal. Remember, what you write is for your eyes only. You may at some time choose to share what you have written with someone. However, I believe you will be less likely to censor if you are writing for your eyes-only.

Daily Practices

Day One: What is something(s) that you have not been completely honest with yourself and/or others regarding your relationships?

Day Two: What is something(s) that you have not been completely honest with yourself and/or others regarding your health or health practices?

Day Three: What is something(s) that you have not been completely honest with yourself and/or others regarding your career?

Day Four: What is something(s) that you have not been completely honest with yourself and/or others regarding your spiritual life and/or adherence to my own moral standards?

Day Five: Identify ways that you compromised that lead to being less of yourself? Keep in mind the positive aspects of who you are, goals, dreams or aspirations you have let go in the name of compromise?

Day Six: Identify something(s) you have done that you would not want anyone one else to know about or you have never share with anyone?

Day Seven: Based on this week's exercises, is there anything you could do to show up more fully in your life, such as transcend feelings of guilt or feel more authentic with yourself or others?

43. Loving kindness

"Before you speak, ask yourself, is it kind, is it necessary, and is it true, does it improve on the silence?"

—Shirdi Sai Baba, Indian saint

Sometimes it feels like everyone is angry with everyone else. A prevailing lack of caring and concern has become commonplace. Courtesy and friendliness have become a thing of the past only making an appearance at times of extreme national tragedies. It almost feels like a litigious society has become the standard for behavior with everyone rushing to judge everyone else. There seems to be a strong need to be right, to be first and to get the goods on the other guy. Aggression has become the norm. I guess that's why I was delightfully surprised when I saw the movie "Pay It Forward" starring Kevin Spacey, Helen Hunt and Haley Joel Osmet. The film was released with comparatively little promotion and fanfare by current Hollywood advertising standards. It was a popular favorite however, if you consider word of mouth recommendations from numerous moviegoers. The film was enjoyed and experienced by many as a "breath of fresh air." in a sea of dark motion picture fare filled with violence and aggression. The central theme of the movie was about a child who does good deeds, random acts of kindness for others without them knowing. They, in turn, would do acts of kindness for others until the cumulative effect was felt and miracles began to happen.

Recently, I read about some real life random acts of kindness in the newspaper. Some were heroic and others were stories of good people doing really good things. I enjoyed reading these articles since it supports my belief in the genuine goodness of human beings. However, my enthusiasm was tempered by the realization of a paradox. I realized that only those stories considered out of the ordinary make the news because that's what sells newspapers. I thought, "How truly sad that the occasional random acts of kindness make news." This is not a good sign. It either means random acts of kindness are trivialized and used as fillers on light news days, or, in fact, they are so rare as to become newsworthy.

Soon after having this awakening I saw another headline that read, "The Angry Side of Disease". The story was about people that are told by their doctor they have a serious medical problem. The person featured in the article talked about the difficulty she had dealing with the news of her life threatening diagnosis and the fact that people around her didn't suddenly stop cutting in line, bad drivers didn't stop swerving in front of her, and the obnoxious didn't automatically begin to behave better. The world didn't magically turn soft and fuzzy. As I read this article I began to think about the times in my life when the challenges were overwhelming and I felt so raw emotionally that even another car coming close to mine was cause for extreme tension and stress. I began to think about all the people I met in the past week that were strangers who might have been suffering some kind of physical and/or emotional pain. I wondered if I had interacted with them in a kind way or with aggression. I wanted to be able to go back in time, to have another chance to relive the encounter and make sure it had a good outcome.

We all recall times in our life when we were particularly vulnerable and someone was unkind and thoughtless. We can relate to how it felt. We can also recall times when we have been unkind, short and abrupt with others without a thought to what they might be going through. I think at times like these we are given an opportunity to see more clearly and recognize how things can be different. It's an opportunity for change. That is not to say you won't get angry, but you can reject aggressive reactions and respond more thoughtfully. You can learn to listen to other points of view without jumping to conclusions and trying to overpower and over talk others with anger and aggression. You can temper your responses until you've given yourself time to think things through. You can ask yourselves if it is really necessary to take the issues to an arena filled with aggression. Realize that you can choose a response based in the practice of loving kindness to reach a harmonious solution. You can choose to incorporate loving kindness into all your encounters as a life changing choice with the goal of bringing peace to yourself and others. You can choose to merge random acts of kindness with loving kindness as a way of life. This means choosing to keep peace in your heart and respond to conflict within yourself and with others in a loving non-aggressive way.

It begins with making the conscious decision to practice being compassionate in all your interactions. You decide to bring peace into your own life by being compassionate and loving toward yourself. Then you extend that compassionate loving kindness to your interactions with others. If you are intrigued by the possibility of living a life of peace and harmony and want to give yourself the gift of freedom gained

Dr. Mike Davison, Kay Guzder

by incorporating loving kindness into your life, start by asking yourself these questions?

Am I impoverished emotionally because I lack loving kindness toward myself?

Can I commit to practicing loving kindness toward myself as the first step in eliminating the acts of aggression I commit against myself and others?

Can I cultivate compassion and open my heart and mind to my own suffering and the suffering of others?

Can I commit to living my life as an instrument of peace?

These questions may have stirred some strong emotions in you. If they did, and you want to take some action that will lead you toward the path that beings peace back into your life, start with extending loving kindness to yourself. By viewing the challenges of life through the gentle lens of loving kindness, you can empower yourself. By practicing loving kindness when you find yourself embroiled in an angry encounter you free yourself from the stress and tension associated with aggression. As you practice loving kindness and experience it as a way of life, you will be able to "pay it forward" to others. In doing so you join with those who are an active force for peace and together you become a guiding light to others who wish to break free from the destructive web of aggression.

"We can either let the situations of our lives harden our hearts or we can use them to enlarge our hearts, to strengthen our compassion, to build our spiritual fortitude."

—*Pema Chodron*

Daily Practices

Day One: Spend some time reflecting and journaling on what you think about yourself. How do you treat yourself? Are you frequently judgmental and negative about yourself? Are you critical, harsh and fault finding? Do you practice loving kindness toward yourself? Write a few paragraphs in your journal answering these questions in detail.

Day Two: After reviewing yesterday's journal entries reflect on ways you want to change how you think about yourself. Write a plan in your journal about the steps you want to begin to incorporate acts of loving kindness into your self care..

Day Three and Four: Reflect on your perception and treatment of others, those who are well known to you and those who are strangers. Spend some time journaling about some ways you would like to change how you interact in your relationships with others to incorporate acts of loving kindness in your daily interactions. Write some specific ideas on how you can extend this practice to your family, friends and strangers. Include a sentence about how soon you intend to begin "paying it forward".

Day Five: Spend some time reflecting on the concept of extending loving kindness to yourself and others. Write a few paragraphs in your journal about the benefits you will receive from incorporating the practice into your life.

Day Six: Spend some time reflecting and journaling about how you could have used loving kindness in some past conflicted situations to achieve a better outcome for yourself and others.

Day Seven: Write a plan of action about how you will

practice loving kindness in your interactions over the next seven days. Spend a few minutes every day writing about what you learned as the result of offering the gift of loving kindness to yourself and others.

44. Addition by subtraction

"Identify the things that drain you and eliminate them—people, places, and things—once and for all."

—Cheryl Richardson

A friend and mentor of mine, John DiLemme, introduced me to the concept of "addition by subtraction". My sense of what he meant was that a quality life involves not only adding things and developing new healthy ritual, but also means "cleaning house". This is important in the area of relationships. Do you have toxic people in your life? Do you have people in your life that are on a different and perhaps incompatible path? You only have one life to live. You may as well make it as happy, meaningful and filled with peace as you can. Don't waste your time with people who are consumed with negativity. This is not a judgment. Wish them well, but do it from a distance. I refer to folks like this as emotional vampires or dream stealers. They are fueled by having an audience to view their life's drama unfolding. They are folks that are addicted to the drama, addicted to their victim story.

I hope I am not losing anyone here. I know there are people who have experienced unthinkable things in their life.

However, even when blame is "justified", it is not productive to stay stuck in it. I am also not referring to folks that are going through a temporary challenge in life. I am specifically referring to people that have this as their way of life. They walk around with a bull's eye on their shirt and seem to chase down slaps in the face. They can be described as injustice collectors.

Some may feel that it sounds harsh to just turn your back on a person with such an orientation to the world. You may not have to. You can allow a safe port to dock for them, without that dock becoming a permanent home. Everyone one has problems and challenges, but not everyone allows them to rule them. Not everyone organizes their identity and unfolding life story around them. Remember the advice that is given prior to take off on a commercial airplane. If the plane is in distress place the oxygen mask on yourself first and your child second. If you can't take care of yourself, you are no good to anyone else. If you have relationships with people who drain you or find it unacceptable to allow you to care for yourself, it is time to re-evaluate that relationship.

This week's practices can create short-term discomfort for some. Remember, this process is ultimately about cultivating a greater sense of personal peace. Keep this outcome in mind. Also please be mindful that cultivating your spiritual condition involves being loving and gentle with yourself. You may identify people or "things" that are draining you. However, it does not mean you have to take action on that today. You can start with the areas that you think will potentially be easier, and save the ones you think will be tougher for later in the week.

Daily Practices

Day One: You will have more energy if you are comfortable with your physical surroundings. Use your journal to identify things you may need to get rid off (example: clothes you don't wear anymore), areas you may need to clean up (example: garage, car, junk draw, office), and areas you need to organize (example: your system for bill paying).

Day Two: Identify what the benefits would be if you made the changes identified above?

Day Three: You will have more energy and feel more spiritually nourished when you modify or eliminate certain activities in your life. Use your journal to identify unhealthy things you ingest, or ingest too much of (examples caffeine, alcohol, cigarettes, junk food, prescription medications, drugs) and activities you spend too much time involved in (examples surfing the net, watching TV, video games).

Day Four: Identify what the benefits would be if you made the changes identified above?

Day Five: This one may be a bit tougher than day one and day two. You will feel more fulfilled and spiritually alive in life when you spend time with people who are supportive of your emotional, physical and spiritual well being. Use your journal to answer the following questions:

> I would describe the way I get along with my siblings as…
>
> I would describe the way I get along with my extended family as…
>
> I would describe the way I get along with people at work as…
>
> I would describe the way I get along with my spouse as…

Dr. Mike Davison, Kay Guzder

I would describe the way I get along with my children as...

I would describe the way I get along with my neighbors as...

I would describe the way I get along with my friends as...

Day Six: Based on your work yesterday, are there specific people who you need to modify in some way your relationship with. Keep in mind that by modifying it can mean anything from minor changes to ending the relationship.

Day Seven: Identify what the benefits would be if you made the changes in your relationships you identified above?

Section VII. Widening & Deepening Your Path of Personal Peace

45. Positive mental attitude

Believe in yourself! Have faith in your abilities! Without a humble but reasonable confidence in your own powers you cannot be successful or happy.

—Norman Vincent Peale

The motivational literature abounds with references to keeping a Positive Mental Attitude (PMA). Having a PMA is about allowing yourself to be guided by faith and a quest for continuous personal and spiritual improvement. The dominant focus of individuals with a PMA is on the present moment. This is not inconsistent with having goals for the future, however their dominate focus is on the present moment. Too much focus on the future can fuel a sense of discouragement and doubt that will block true personal peace.

As mentioned above, having a PMA means having a deep faith and a deep sense of knowing. That does not mean that you will always achieve your outcomes. However, faith means you will get the outcome that you need to help you to get to the next level on your spiritual journey.

Your attitude, or your willingness to think positively, affects many people—from your family to the stranger you smile at in the grocery store. Cultivating optimism will help you see opportunity in difficulties, while pessimism will lock you into the mode of seeing difficulty in opportunities. Pessimism is counter to PMA and personal peace.

You must choose what you will focus on in any situation. If you choose to focus on obstacles and negativity, you will doom yourself to never achieving your goals or the personal peace which is your birthright.

So how do you begin to think positively if you are a natural pessimist? People aren't natural pessimists, they are people who have trained themselves to consider the darkest side of every cloud.

You cannot change the fact that challenges will arise from time-to-time, but you can do a lot to determine what opportunity lies within any given challenge. Begin to see that bumps in the road are a fact of life and that your job is to find a way over, around, under, or through them—as quickly as possible. When you're upbeat and consider how quickly a problem will be behind you, it's easy to be optimistic.

Cynicism is another killer when it comes to attitude. It is a cousin of pessimism—it considers everything suspect and everyone as having an ulterior motive. It never looks at someone handing you a piece of candy just to be nice, it always considers that there is a reason you're being handed the candy and the motivation of the person who is giving it.

Cynicism comes from having unrealistic expectations. Many people expect great and wonderful things to happen to them with little-to-no work on their part. They expect things to fall from the sky in to their laps. When it doesn't happen as they expect, they become suspicious of others who have achieved success and ultimately feel discouraged, defeated and cynical.

You must harness the power of your thoughts and the words you use when communicating with yourself and others in your spiritual journey. Use positive affirmations daily: remind yourself that a stumbling block is temporary and that you will overcome it; admit to yourself that you are courageous and able to move on when others cannot; agree with the vision you have for your life.

As you discipline yourself to do this, you will find optimism and positive thinking all around you. Couldn't you use these two friends when you are aiming for a life of success and personal peace?

Daily Practices

Day One: The great motivationalist, W. Clement Stone wrote: "No matter who you are you can have a Magnificent Obsession". What does having a positive attitude, or a "Magnificent Obsession" have to do with being more spiritual? Journal your thoughts.

The next Three days of practices will invovle contemplating quotes from Norman Vincent Peale. Use your journal to capture your reflections.

Day Two: "People become really quite remarkable when they start thinking that they can do things. When they believe in themselves they have the first secret of success.

If you want to get somewhere you have to know where you want to go and how to get there. Then never, never, never give up."—Peale

Day Three: "The "how" thinker gets problems solved effectively because he wastes no time with futile "ifs" but goes right to work on the creative "how.""—Peale

Day Four: "Cut the "im" out of impossible, leading that dynamic word standing out free and clear—possible."—Peale

Day Five: "The positive thinker is a hard-headed, tough-minded, and factual realist. He sees all the difficulties clearly... which is more than can be said for the average negative thinker. But he sees more than difficulties—he tries to see the solutions of those difficulties."—Peale

Day Six: A daily mantra W. Clement Stone recommended for positive self-suggestion was:

"I feel healthy! I feel happy! I feel terrific!" Shout this out loudly several times today.

Day Seven: Reflect upon this week's practices on developing a PMA. As in day one, identify what having a positive attitude has to do with spirtiuality? How can having a positive mental attitude help you attract more of what you want in the world?

46. Gratitude

Ask yourself, "Are you coming from abundance or deprivation"?

—Sarah Ban Breathnach

If you look around on any given day you will be able to identify people who are visibly unhappy. They move through life as if each day is a battle. Every encounter is experienced as something they must win or lose and every loss is internalized and personalized. Operating with this mindset allows them to add to their storage bank of negative experiences and pull up endless justifications for their sour outlook on life. The process of selective perception lets them see themselves as victims of circumstance. It imprisons them in a world of negativity. In order to maintain this negative belief system, they have to ignore wide areas of their lives that are positive as they focus on things that aren't the way they want them to be. It takes a lot of energy to work that hard and find reasons to be unhappy and dissatisfied. While most of us don't have this extreme degree of negativity, we do take some of life's gifts and pleasures for granted, often missing the real joy of living with an "attitude of gratitude".

Author, Sara Breathnach, in her book *Simple Abundance*, gives us many reminders of the daily blessings we have in our lives. She suggests we ask the question "Are you coming from abundance or deprivation?" Living your life with an "attitude of gratitude" has a lot to offer. Author Melody Beattie writes; "Gratitude unlocks the fullness of life. It turns what we have into enough, and more. It turns denial into acceptance, chaos into order, and confusion to clarity. Gratitude makes sense of our past, brings peace for today, and creates a vision for tomorrow." There are abundant gifts and benefits available for those who seek personal peace by cultivating an attitude of gratitude.

Think about a time when you felt a deep sense of gratitude. Perhaps a memory of a Thanksgiving dinner you shared with family or friends comes to mind. Often before eating we spend time telling one another why we are grateful. I've noticed at these times, people don't normally talk about material things. They focus on the true meaningful gifts of life. More likely they express gratitude for family and friends, good health, the beauty of nature, and so on. As I write, I am reminded of my family's Thanksgiving dinner of November, 2001, two months after the tragic events of September 11th. As we sat around the table I heard the young adults expressing their cynicism about the state of the world. They were finding it difficult to remain optimistic and were concerned about their future. Their attempts at gratitude were half hearted. As luck would have it, I had time earlier in the day to read the newspaper and found an editorial that suggested some unique reasons for being grateful that Thanksgiving Day. It asked the reader to reflect, "If you awakened today to read the newspaper you need to be grateful. If you have two eyes to read the newspaper, be grateful. If you have only one eye to read the newspaper, feel grateful that you still have one good eye. If you have both your hands to hold the newspaper, be grateful. If you only have one hand, then you can still put it down on the table and turn the pages, be grateful. If you have a table and food to put on it and friends and family to share it with, you have ample reason to be grateful." The editorial brought the real gifts of life into sharp focus. I saved it to read at the table when it was my turn to share and express my gratitude. I expected my family to respond either with silence or a grateful "Amen, let's eat". But that didn't happen. Apparently the newspaper article had a profound impact. It was just what was needed to counter the cynicism and hopeless feelings at the sad state of affairs in the world and refocus on the simple gifts that life offers on a daily basis. The young adults came to the table sad and discouraged, worried about the possibility of war and unsure about their future. They voiced concern about finding jobs after graduating from college. They no longer felt protected and safe. Rarely had they ever experienced such feelings of personal discouragement and vulnerability before. They began to realize their lives had been rather sheltered, most of their concerns centering around their social life or on term papers that were due. They felt ill prepared to deal with the reality of life after September 11th, and felt adrift in unknown seas. They longed to feel anchored. The thought provoking editorial got them thinking about the important gifts in their lives.

There was silence for a while after I read the edotorial. Then, one by one, people began to share in a more meaningful way why they were grateful. The conversation became hopeful and positive. I witnessed a profound transition that day. In the process of verbalizing an attitude of gratitude, the young adults were able to focus on the possibilities their futures held and became optimistic and grateful. They refocused their energy that Thanksgiving Day and realized they were blessed with abundance and the true gifts of life.

I have the impression that a lot of unhappy people have the

perception of being cheated or starved in some way. They seem to maintain a very grasping posture toward life. They feel miserable because they think that life is not giving them what they need. Their stranglehold on life keeps them desperately trying to wring out the love and satisfaction they crave. Sadly they choke off the supply that is life-sustaining. Gratitude tells us there is enough for everyone and most of us have more than we really need. If you can identify with these unhappy folks, perhaps you are open to some self discovery. Think about turning inward to the wellspring of your life. You have an infinite supply of love and happiness within you. It doesn't work to search elsewhere and depend on others to make you happy. You have the ability to create your own personal "attitude of gratitude" and it resides in you. Think about that newspaper article and ask yourself what is really causing you to feel deprived and then make a list of all the gifts in your life for which you are grateful. Experience the freedom this simple writing exercise brings you. You will be freed of the negative energy and able to focus on what is within your reach to bring about positive change. Begin by appreciating all that you are, all that you have, and all that you can be.

Daily Practices

Day One: Reflect and journal about the things you are most grateful for in your life.

Day Two: Spend some time writing about people and things you may have taken for granted that you now realize are gifts to be treasured.

Day Three: Write about the gifts you see in nature that you have ignored or not noticed in the past. This exercise will help you learn to "slow down and smell the roses."

Day Four: Reflect for a while about a time when you were cynical and couldn't find anything to be grateful for. How long did you stay stuck in that negative mindset? How did you get beyond that episode of cynicism? What was the outcome?

Day Five: Spend some time writing in your journal about the way you feel when you view your life and environment with an attitude of gratitude. Write specifically about how you will let others know that you are grateful they are part of your life.

Day Six: Reflect on the ordinary things in your life for which you are grateful. Write a few paragraphs about how to stay focused on these gifts of abundance the next time you feel challenged and start to feel negative and cynical.

Day Seven: Spend some time reflecting and journaling about how an attitude of gratitude gives birth to joyful living.

47. The good, the bad, and the ugly: Embracing your imperfections

"Perfectionism is not about doing one's best, or about pursuing excellence; it's about the emotional conviction that perfection is the only route to personal acceptance. It is the emotional conviction that by being perfect, one can finally be acceptable as a person."

—Dr. Tom Greenspon

I love an inspirational film. One of my favorites is "Rudy". There is a brilliant scene where Rudy is deeply discouraged and is in church looking rather defeated. Rudy asks a priest for some advice and reassurance to which the priest responds brilliantly. To paraphrase, the priest responds to Rudy by saying that in his 35 years of being a priest he is only sure of two things. One is that there is a God. The second is that he is not God. That scene is a humble reminder of our imperfection as human beings. The great psychologist, Alfred Adler, felt that all humans have what he refers to as feelings of inferiority or imperfection. He also sees these feelings of inferiority as a core motivator that explains much of our behavior. Much of our behavior, according to Adler, can be explained as striving to overcome feelings of inferiority.

The key is that we continue to strive, to strive for perfection, with the courage to be imperfect. Having a goal of actually being perfect just creates needless stress. Perfectionism leaves individuals devoid of personal peace, mainly because perfection is an impossible goal. I have heard it said that perfectionism is the lowest of all standards. That is because it is unachievable and often leads to a lack of goal directed behavior. It is a sure way of defeating oneself before even starting.

Now, now, I must emphasize that I am not promoting low standards. I am suggesting having clear goals, being determined and persistent with a spirit of accepting that humanness. Being human is to be imperfect. The quest for perfection contributes to stress, medical complications, a lack of serenity and contaminated relationships. Forget about the motivational literature that suggests giving 110%. Not only is that bad math, it contributes to the opposite effect; blocking the avenue to the inner peace and joy you are seeking.

The practices this week will involve contemplative writing exercises. Each day read the passage and silently contemplate on it. Upon completion of your silent contemplation, write about what the passage means to you. Keep in mind that knowledge itself is meaningless, applied knowledge changes lives.

Daily Practices

Day One: "It doesn't matter what we do until we accept ourselves. Once we accept ourselves, it doesn't matter what we do."

—Charly Heavenrich

Day Two: "Self-acceptance comes from meeting life's challenges vigorously. Don't numb yourself to your trials and difficulties, nor build mental walls to exclude pain from your life. You will find peace not by trying to escape your problems, but by confronting them courageously. You will find peace not in denial, but in victory".

—Donald Walters

Day Three: "By accepting you as you are, I do not necessarily abandon all hope of your improving."

—Ashleigh Brilliant

Day Four: "Better to do something imperfectly than to do nothing flawlessly."

—Robert Schuller

Day Five: "Ring the bells that still can ring,
forget your perfect offering.
There's a hole in everything,
that's how the light comes thru."

—Leonard Cohen

Day Six: "A child becomes an adult when he realizes that he has a right not only to be right but also to be wrong."

—Thomas Szasz

Day Seven:

Mary Oliver A segment from her poem "Wild Geese"

You do not have to be good.
You do not have to walk on your knees
for a hundred miles through the desert repenting.
You only have to let the soft animal of your body
love what it loves.

Tell me about despair, yours, and I will tell you mine.
Meanwhile the world goes on.
Meanwhile the sun and the clear pebbles of the rain
are moving across the landscapes,
over the prairies and the deep trees,
the mountains and the rivers.
Meanwhile the wild geese, high in the clean blue air,
are heading home again.

Whoever you are, no matter how lonely,
the world offers itself to your imagination,
calls to you like the wild geese, harsh and exciting—
over and over announcing your place
in the family of things.

48. Faith versus fear

Good sound advice I have heard many times in my life is "Don't worry about it." If only it was that easy. An extraordinary life is not one without fear. In my way of thinking, a successful life is one in which people experience fear and act out of faith. I have a dear friend who is extraordinarily successful in every domain of life. I admire him so much. A great deal of my admiration comes not only from seeing what he has been able to achieve in all areas of his life, but where he came from. I have known him long enough that I know when things were not going as well for him. I admire all that he overcame.

In speaking with him one day, I was picking his brain about how he has been able to achieve all that he has been able to achieve. I ask him how he has been able to free himself of fear. He quickly responded that he can't remember a day he has not been fearful and uncomfortable. His response was rather shocking to me. I had assumed that he was free of anxiety, which is what helped him achieve the amazing outcomes in his life. He went on to explain to me that he views fear as an emotion which can disable him or an emotion that he can act through by having a deep sense of faith.

When I asked him to expand this mindset, he went on to

Dr. Mike Davison, Kay Guzder

share how having an overriding outcome for each area of his life keeps him moving forward. He embraced a philosophy that indicated that people are best understood not by where they were coming from, but what they were moving toward, the bigger the vision, the greater the discomfort. However, the more compelling the vision is, the more desire there will be to pursue it in spite of fear or discomfort.

My friend went on to speak of his faith in God. He shared a Bible verse that has been meaningful to him, which is "Give all your worries and cares to God, for he cares what happens to you" (1 Peter 5:7). He stated that he finds much comfort in the idea that instead of worrying, he can hand his problems over to the care of God. He shared how this was not at all a passive statement about the role he needed to play in his own life. He stated that he knows today that God helps those who do their part AND ask Him for help. My friend clearly derives a great sense of certainty and courage in the knowledge that God can and will care for him in perfect ways.

I encourage you, as I encourage myself, to take the perspective of my friend in being willing to transfer your fears and worries to the only One who truly can solve them and bring a greater sense of ease to your anxious moments. That, is true personal peace.

Exercises

Day 1: What situations evoke the most fear in your life at this time?

Day 2: Of the circumstances that evoke the most fear for you, which ones can you personally change? What are the ones over which you have no control?

Day 3: What are your "natural tendencies" when you are fearful?

Day 4: Are there any pay offs for being fearful and allowing fear to limit your forward movement?

Day 5: Do you know someone who seems to have little to no observable fear? What is it the helps them move forward in spite of fear or discomfort in their life?

Day 6: What does it mean to turn your worries and fears over to the care of God? How does one do this?

Day 7: What is one situation that you can and you will place in God's hands today?

49. Taking stock

"I can give you a six word formula for success. Think things through—then follow through."

—Edward Rickenbacker, aviator (1890-1973)

As with any journey into new territory it is important now and then to take a look at a road map to see how far you have traveled, where you are at present, and where you want to end up. It is no less important on your journey toward finding personal peace that you take stock of what you have learned along the way. Some ideas being presented may be familiar to you and you may find you are less focused on them. Others philosophies and ideas may be new and take some time to grasp. In either case, it is a good idea to take stock on a regular basis to see if you are making progress. Have you been able to incorporate some of the changes into your life that you had in mind when you began your journey? Perhaps now is a good time to examine whether you have made any headway or if you are still stuck in the old ways?

As you take some time to get your bearings and think about your journey, perhaps you will make the discovery that you have accomplished more than you realized. Perhaps you have applied some ideas that appealed to you. It could be that a particular story had significance for you. Maybe you'll find that you want to learn more about yourself by focusing more on the daily practices and journaling regularly. This is a good time to review and renew your commitment to bring peaceful resolutions to your conflicts as a way of finding personal peace. There is value in finding out if you are as far along in your journey as you would like to be. Ask yourself if you need to take steps to get "unstuck, stop spinning your wheels and get back on track again".

In this chapter the daily practices will help you "think things through—then follow through". Take stock and see if you want to make some shifts and changes on your road map or corrections in your guideposts. Go ahead a tailor your trip to meet your needs. Be sure to journal how you are going to celebrate what you have accomplished up till now, for it is in starting the journey in the first place that gives us a sense of direction and joy. And as Ben Sweetland, an inspirational writer, tells us, "Success is a journey, not a destination." Enjoy your journey you will find peace along the way.

Daily Practices

Day One: Journal about why you started on this journey. Where were you stuck at the time, what did you want to change?

Day Two: How have the daily practices helped you?

Day Three: What chapters helped you? What ideas and concepts appealed to you?

Day Four: What would you like to improve? What else would you like to change?

Day Five: What is better now than when you started?

Day Six: What changes have you made? Finish this sentence: My life is different because I…

Write the answer in your journal.

Day Seven: Write your own motto for keeping yourself on track. What helps you to stay the course? Write some words of encouragement to yourself about your accomplishments so far. Then write about what you want to change and what you want to move toward. What do you need to concentrate on or modify to reach your goals?

> "Shoot for the moon. Even if you miss it you will land among the stars."
>
> —*Les Brown, motivational speaker, writer.*

50. Congruence is key

Subtlety may deceive you; integrity never will.

—Oliver Cromwell

What does it mean to be a congruent person? Generically it means you have aligned your behavior with your core values and life's purpose. Some people refer to this as living in integrity. It is the highest form of honesty. A highly congruent person (the 100% congruent person does not exist) is authentically living their life and is living their truth in the world. They don't have shameful secrets to hide. Their life is an open book. As they say in the recovery movement, "you are only as sick as your secrets". Highly congruent people have no secrets.

Living with a high level of congruence also allows people to prioritize their decision-making. For example, a person of integrity who places a high value on the sanctity of marriage will not put them self in a situation that increases their temptation to have an affair.

Living in congruence means living in complete honesty. It means being principle centered and adhering to the principles. As mentioned in a previous week, we debunked the notion of a person obtaining a state of perfection. However,

Dr. Mike Davison, Kay Guzder

people of congruence are quick to acknowledge when they are out of integrity and are act promptly to re-align themselves.

We live in a world where integrity is becoming a higher value. Some may disagree, however evidence in the world of business suggests that this is the case. The Enron's and WorldCom's of the world are no longer tolerated. Seemingly every month another company topples because of the acts of deception and lack of integrity.

The benefits of living in integrity are endless. One of the benefits is having the feeling of calmness and well-being that comes from being open and honest about all of your actions. Your relationships will be based on trust and not suspicion. You will be a high standard or model of integrity to your children, your friends, your business associates, and to all that you encounter. Additionally, if you receive accolades from others it will feel genuine and well deserved. Most of all, living your life in a congruent manner will allow you to achieve the highest level of personal peace.

What does all of this mean in a practical sense? It means that you will put the right philosophy (the golden rule) into practice in all that you do. You will not step on someone else to climb the "ladder of success". Make a commitment to treat people with respect, honesty, and trust. Behave toward others how you want (and expect) them to behave toward you.

Be a model of "doing the right thing" to those around you. When you live you life with integrity you realize what are the most important things in life.

For those with children, an important thing to be mindful of as you consider living a life of congruence, character and integrity is that your children will grow up to be just like you. John Maxwell once wrote, "We teach what we know;

we reproduce who we are." So as a person who is full of integrity and character, you will reproduce those same traits in your children (and others in your circle of influence) as you allow your best life to unfold. Isn't that really what it's all about, anyhow?

Daily Practices

Day One: Part of living a congruent life means knowing your core values. What do you value most in life? Place the values below (those that apply to you) in sequential order. Also include values that are not listed if they come to mind.

Gratitude
Love
Passion
Contribution
Confidence
Security
Excitement
Approval
Achievement
Recognition
Happiness
Growth
Respect
Creativity
Adventure
Making a Difference
Acceptance
Success
Intelligence
Courage
List your top 5:

Day Two: What emotional states would you most like to avoid? Like in yesterdays practice, place them in sequential order. Don't limit yourself to those listed.

Away from Values:
Anger
Rejection
Fear
Physical Pain
Depression
Humiliation
Indecision
Unloved
Loneliness
Embarrassment
Unappreciated
Impatience
Failure
Jealousy
Dishonesty
Stress
Defensiveness
Negativity
Denial
Laziness
Inferiority

List your top 5:

Day Three: What do you make of the moving toward and moving away from values you identified in the first two days of practices? What does this say about you?

Day Four: Reflect on the values you identify in day one and two. How consistent have your actions been with your stated values? How do you feel when your behavior is not aligned with your values?

Day Five: Martin Luther King, Jr. wrote: "The time is always right to do what is right". Use your journal to reflect on what his statement means to you?

Day Six: Zig Ziglar, the famous motivational speaker wrote: "Good values are easier caught than taught". What does this mean to you? Are you hitting the mark in the area of modeling the values to those who mean the most to you?

Day Seven: What daily exercise or ritual can you create in your life to help you align your behavior with your values?

51. The Deming way

Commit to CANI!—Constant And Never-ending Improvement.

—Tony Robbins

Dr. Deming is most known for his impact on the field of manufacturing and quality control. Coming from an engineering background he has been credited for having a major impact in transforming manufacturing in Japan. His basic principles are simple, yet profound. It flies in the face of the commonly held notion of "If it ain't broke, don't fix it". Deming promoted a philosophy of always striving for improvement.

While Deming worked in business, his principles are easily transferred to our personal lives. The consciousness of continual improvement is key to obtaining and sustaining personal peace in your life. It involves constantly seeking ways to improve yourself in all areas of your life. In Japan they have a term for this concept of never ending improvement. The term is "kaizen". It is based on the notion that progress and success comes out of the mindset of continually examining and training and improving. Think of how the concept of never ending improvement can apply to your spiritual journey. You can examine your life across the board and examine how you can be a "slightly" better spouse, parent, employee, friend, or "slightly" improve in any domain of your life. This mindset is important, particularly when taken with a broad perspective. In my work with hundreds of people over the years I have seen many folks who are highly lopsided in their development. For example, they may be highly developed in their professional life yet poorly developed in their physical health, marriage, or recreational life.

To truly implement the concept of Kaisen there needs to be willingness to continual self-examination. It also requires a commitment to your spiritual journey. Take each of your goals or each of the areas of your life and ask yourself the question "How can this be improved by one percent". Remember your spiritual path is a long and winding road. Tiny changes over time can lead to profound change over time. The mindset of Kaisen is also respectful to how we are wired neurologically and the brilliance of making small incremental changes. While the motivational literature abounds with thoughts of making giant changes overnight, this approach can backfire. Rapid change can activate the emotional center of the brain and contribute to pulling back into the land of familiar.

Overall I believe you should have high ideals for yourself in your spiritual journey. However, like a high jumper, you can slowly raise the bar over time. But…remember to raise the bar.

This week's practices will help you use small incremental changes to create profound long-term change in your life. A mindset I want to promote is amplified in Robert Mauer's book "One Small Step Can Change Your Life: The Kaizen Way". Some of these ideas were summarized by a friend of mine Karen Purves. Karen's summary points include:

* Focus on making small steps for continual improvement. Make the steps small and comfortable.

* The steps should be really small—"almost embarrassingly trivial at first."

* This way you master the smallest steps of change in a safe, non-threatening environment. The fear mechanism in your brain is not activated this way. That is the key.

* Small steps gets you out of being "stuck" and bypasses the brains fight or flight response.

* Ask small questions—even to change big issues or problems.

* Remember when you are reprogramming your brain; it takes time for new neural pathways to develop.

* Sometimes you can start with things as little as thinking something 15 seconds a day and not doing anything differently.

* If you are resisting something, make the step even smaller.

* Train yourself to focus on the small, positive aspects of your partner.

* Recent studies suggest "that people who respond to life's challenges with anger are seven times more likely to die prematurely from heart disease than those with the same lifestyle but different temperament."

In carrying out the practices this week, remember to use the kind and gentle approach of making small incremental shifts. Specifically this week the practices will emphasize making a small shift in a number of areas that will help you develop self-care rituals that will strengthen your spiritual condition and increase your experience of personal peace.

Daily Practices

Day One: The balance of sleep and wakefulness.

Sleep and wakefulness are absolutely fundamental to creating balance in life. If you sleep too much and you become lethargic, unmotivated and depressed and are out of balance If you sleep too little and you become forgetful, edgy, irritable and impatient you are out of balance. Sleeping is an inhibitory process that allows your brain to become refreshed and renewed for the next day's activity. Sleep can be disturbed by day-to-day over-stimulation, and by under-stimulation.

Identify one small shift you can make in this area:

Day Two: The balance of movement and rest.

Research has shown that daily movement such as an exercise program, walking or manual labor can lower blood pressure, decrease heart rate, improve cognitive function and increase well being. Movement counteracts the inevitable physical tension that results from sustained mental activity. It does so at the deepest level of the nervous system, where physical inactivity, combined with vigilant, mental activation is equated with danger.

Identify one small shift you can make in this area:

Day Three: The balance of relationships and being alone:

Directly or indirectly, we are constantly in contact with others. It is a stimulating experience that evokes strong reactions from deep within our brains and our hearts. Too much of this contact is virtual, through television, the Internet, and over the telephone lines and not enough is in person, with people to whom we have strong connections. Virtual contact with others through electronic means usually occurs when you are alone. Then, your nervous system becomes stimulated by visceral, emotional reactions without the calming structure of an in-person relationship. Time alone must be balanced by time spent with real life, in person, contact with people.

Identify one small shift you can make in this area:

Day Four: The balance of emotion and intellect.

Your brain works through a dynamic balance between emotion and intellect. Emotion is an excitatory process that powers action, memory and thought. Intellectual activity or thought is an inhibitory process, where the brain, to inhibit, time, modify and plan action, manipulates mental images and symbols. The visceral aspects of emotion, the energy of emotion, come from the older parts of the brain in the limbic system and subcortical areas. Intellectual thought comes from the newer, neocortex, primarily in the frontal lobes. These two areas of the brain are hard-wired together because the balance of emotion and thought is fundamental to proper brain activity. Too little emotion and you become flattened, dull, withdrawn and unhappy. Too little intellectual thought and you become labile, reactive and over-emotional, ultimately burned out and depressed.

Identify one small shift you can make in this area:

Day Five: The balance of past and present and future.

Finding the right balance with you orientation to time is essential. We need some time to review our past, but too much time can be ingredients for depression. We need some time to plan for the future, but spending too much time there can sap your enjoyment in the present by creating too much anticipatory anxiety. Being in the present brings the greatest sense of peace and calm.

Identify one small shift you can make in this area:

Day Six: The balance of belief and doubt.

Since the scientific revolution our culture has highly empha-sized doubt and questioning. This is good except when it is not. It can lead to cynicism, worry and anxiety. Newer neu-roimaging studies suggest that our brains are hard-wired to be anxious, worried and doubtful. For example a recent study using MRI imaging found that children with obses-sive-compulsive disorder (a condition of massive worry and anxiety) have an enlarged thalamus—the thalamus is a key, subcortical structure that processes visceral or bodily reac-tions. HOWEVER, worry is effectively counterbalanced by belief. Human beings have long used religious belief as a way to quiet basic worry and doubt. Researchers have shown that belief in a positive outcome can help to rid you of social anxiety, depression and feelings of panic. Believe me!

Identify one small shift you can make in this area:

Day Seven: What area covered this week do you most need to focus on? Develop a game plan that involves a series of small incremental changes to help you develop more solid self-care plans.

52. Commencement

I have participated in a number of commencement ceremonies in my life. I have always found them to be joyous occasions. I particularly enjoy the seeming paradox of a ceremony that marks an ending and a beginning—the close of a chapter and an opening of a new chapter. I see the end of this book in the same light. I hope you see the end of this journey as the beginning of a new chapter in your life. A chapter with a deep commitment to your ongoing emotional and spiritual growth. A life of personal peace.

Achieving and sustaining personal peace requires an ongoing investment and commitment. Even with this commitment, sustaining personal peace will undoubtedly be a challenge at times. Other times personal peace will seem to flow effortlessly in your life. I believe that the moments of flow will be greater as you travel, with commitment, further down your path.

Take some time to review your progress this week. Where have you made gains? Honor those gains. Ask yourself what practices you found yourself wanting to avoid. These are likely the areas you need to dedicate further time and attention to. Remember, Rome wasn't built in a day. A life of personal peace will require the same ongoing effort. Keep in mind that we all have short-comings or challenges that may require ongoing focus and effort. This is not an indication that something is wrong. This is an indication of your humanness. Some look at this as your most important work in life. Learning to tame, work around, and/or transform your personal defects of character or personal vulnerabilities is part of this journey. Take this journey. Embrace this journey.

Daily Practices

Day One: Today review your journal for the practices from days 1-10. What have you learned about yourself? What practices came easy to you? What practices did you find yourself wanting to avoid? What practices do you feel contributed to growth for you? Perhaps most important, what areas do you need to make an ongoing focus?

Day Two: Today review your journal for the practices from days 11-20. What have you learned about yourself? What practices came easy to you? What practices did you find yourself wanting to avoid? What practices do you feel contributed to growth for you? Perhaps most important, what areas do you need to make an ongoing focus?

Day Three: Today review your journal for the practices from days 21-30. What have you learned about yourself? What practices came easy to you? What practices did you find yourself wanting to avoid? What practices do you feel contributed to growth for you? Perhaps most important, what areas do you need to make an ongoing focus?

Day Four: Today review your journal for the practices from days 31-40. What have you learned about yourself? What practices came easy to you? What practices did you find yourself wanting to avoid? What practices do you feel contributed to growth for you? Perhaps most important, what areas do you need to make an ongoing focus?

Day Five: Today review your journal for the practices from days 41-51. What have you learned about yourself? What practices came easy to you? What practices did you find yourself wanting to avoid? What practices do you feel contributed to growth for you? Perhaps most important, what areas do you need to make an ongoing focus?

Day Six: One of my spiritual heroes is Benjamin Franklin. He was a man who had lived his life on purpose. He made contributions in many areas over his life-time. He was also a person who was deeply committed to his personal and spiritual development. He devised a plan that he methodically followed for the last half of his life. A plan to cultivate 13 virtues he cherished and felt were essential to a life of personal peace and serenity.

Based on your review of your journal, what are some of the qualities, characteristics, behaviors or virtues that you feel are essential to cultivate in your life to create sustainable personal peace? Identify the top 10.

Day Seven: Benjamin Franklin's personal and spiritual life plan involved 13 day cycles. Each day he committed himself to cultivating a different virtue. At the end of the 13 day cycle he would simply go back to the beginning. How can you use Benjamin Franklin's approach to develop your own ongoing plan to continue to cultivate personal peace in your life?

About the authors

Dr. Mike Davison is a clinical psychologist with a thriving private practice in Chicago. His interests include the practice of individual psychotherapy, family and couples counseling, organizational consulting, peak performance coaching, and the integration of spirituality and psychotherapy. Dr. Davison also has taught in a doctoral program for clinical psychology since 1996. Dr. Davison lives in Chicago with his wife of 17 years and their three children.

Kay Guzder received her Master's degree in Counseling Psychology from the Adler School of Professional Psychology in Chicago. She has enjoyed a diversified career as a therapist counseling children in two elementary schools in Chicago's inner city. She has provided individual and group therapy to incarcerated adolescents and adults in an Illinois correctional facility. For ten years she maintained a private practice counseling children and adults and facilitating women's support groups. Kay is now retired and enjoys writing, traveling and spending time with her husband of 41 years, her adult son and daughter and her exuberant Chocolate Labrador Retriever, Ty.

You can learn more about Dr. Mike and Kay at www.AnInvitationtoPersonalPeace.com.

www.ingramcontent.com/pod-product-compliance
Lightning Source LLC
Chambersburg PA
CBHW031945090426
42739CB00006B/89